50¢

A CUP OF COMFORT®

for the

Grieving Heart

Stories to lift your spirit
and heal your soul

Edited by
Colleen Sell

D0003697

Aadamsmedia

Avon, Massachusetts

In loving memory of Blanche and James Sell,
Mary and Frank Baum, and Deborah St. Denis

A *Cup of Comfort*® is a registered trademark of F+W Media, Inc.

Published by
Adams Media, a division of F+W Media, Inc.
57 Littlefield Street, Avon, MA 02322 U.S.A.
www.adamsmedia.com and *www.cupofcomfort.com*

ISBN 10: 1-60550-087-9
ISBN 13: 978-1-60550-087-4

Printed in the United States of America.

J I H G F E D C B A

Library of Congress Cataloging-in-Publication Data
is available from the publisher.

This publication is designed to provide accurate and authoritative information with regard to the subject matter covered. It is sold with the
understanding that the publisher is not engaged in rendering legal,
accounting, or other professional advice. If legal advice or other expert
assistance is required, the services of a competent professional person
should be sought.

—From a *Declaration of Principles* jointly adopted by
a Committee of the American Bar Association and
a Committee of Publishers and Associations

Many of the designations used by manufacturers and sellers to distin-
guish their products are claimed as trademarks. Where those designations appear in this book and Adams Media was aware of a trademark
claim, the designations have been printed with initial capital letters.

This book is available at quantity discounts for bulk purchases.
For information, please call 1-800-289-0963.

Contents

Acknowledgments

It is not easy to share one's grief, so I must begin by expressing my gratitude to all those who submitted stories that did not make it into this book.

I am most grateful to the authors whose stories grace these pages. Not only did they provide me with excellent material to begin with, they were also a joy to work with.

As always, my sincere appreciation goes to my colleagues at Adams Media for all they do—and I do mean *all*—especially Meredith O'Hayre, the *Cup of Comfort*® project editor; Paula Munier, who created the *Cup of Comfort*® series; Carol Goff, the book's copyeditor; and Ashley Vierra, the book's designer.

And thanks to my husband Nikk for always being my comforter, my sounding board, and my comic relief.

Introduction

"Your sorrow is your joy unmasked . . . How else can it be? The deeper the sorrow carves into your being, the more joy you can contain."

—Ghandi

I've wanted to do this book for a long time, since spring of 2000, when we were deliberating the topic of the second anthology in the *Cup of Comfort®* series. *Who more than someone grieving the loss of a loved one could use a little comforting?* I'd think. But then I'd fret, *Will we find enough authentic, uplifting, and uniquely personal stories to fill the book?*

I needn't have worried. We received almost three thousand submissions for *A Cup of Comfort® for the Grieving Heart*—every one a touching memoriam to a loved one, each revealing an inspiring and intimate journey through grief. Reading all of those touching portraits of bereavement and narrowing it down to the stories bound between the covers of this book has been one of the most difficult and rewarding experiences of my career. And it brought back memories of my own personal experiences with grief.

When my mother's father died, I was rattled and confused by how hard she grieved for this man who had given her nothing but his name. By her running to the deathbed of this man she had seen exactly three times since her parents' divorce when she was five, each visit initiated by my mom, not by Glen Grimes. Yet, his death devastated her. At ten, I didn't understand, and for years I resented my grandfather for the darkness his death brought into our home. Understanding came decades later. I understand even better now, after compiling this book.

When, two years later, our six-year-old neighbor—the sister of one of my closest friends—died from brain cancer, I was devastated. Heartbroken. And mad. It was the first time in my life that I questioned God. How could he let this happen to Tammy and her family? My grief was minuscule compared to theirs. But they healed, their lives continued, they found joy and happiness again. That was a valuable lesson for me to learn as a young teen.

When my paternal grandfather died, suddenly, of a heart attack while taking a bath as my parents were driving over for a visit, I was several months pregnant with my second child. My parents arrived to find Grandma kneeling over Grandpa's nude body on the bathroom floor, trying to resuscitate him. Dad, who'd been a medic in the Army, took over and managed to revive his father, only to have him crash again. Grandpa crashed and was revived five times. After the fifth, he took my dad's hand in his and said softly, "Let me go, son. It's time. I'm ready to meet our Father." Grandpa's death taught me about the power of faith and love. When he died, the family was almost certain Grandma would soon die, too, of a broken heart. After a sad year or two, she went on to live another twenty-three years, happily and independently for all but the last few, to the age of ninety-three.

When my beloved Grandpa Baum, my mother's stepfather, passed away after a long battle with a litany of ailments, most related to his military career, our family reeled with grief. During that last hospitalization, knowing it would be his last, we each come to say our goodbyes to this gruff-voiced, life-worn New Yorker with a heart of gold. Two weeks before his death, as my two sisters and I had our ten minutes with him in the ICU, he wrote on a small chalk board, "What should I do?" He was referring to a decision whether to have an invasive surgery that might extend his life for a few months, at best. Our answer was unanimous. He had suffered enough. "Do what's best for you, Grandpa. We'll be okay. We'll take care of Grandma." He refused the surgery. Three days before he died, he wrote on the chalkboard, "Take me outside. Want to see sky. Smell ocean." The nursing staff at the VA Hospital, defying regulations, somehow got Grandpa into a wheelchair and took him and all the machinery he was tethered to out onto a deck. It was the most comfortable and relaxing ten minutes he'd had in months.

His wife, my mother's mother, also lived decades as a widow. Her death came slowly and painfully, from Alzheimer's. But at the end, she knew all of us, and for the first time in my memory of her, she was totally at peace.

That is the one thing that all of my deceased family members had in common: as they took their last breath of life, each was at peace. Even Glen Grimes, "God rest his soul," as my mother would say. Even my sister-in-law Debbie, who lost her life to the hideously debilitating disease pancreatic cancer at age forty-three. Much too soon. I had the honor of being a part of Deb's hospice team, and I was holding her hand while her brother and nieces softly sang "Amazing Grace" to her father's accompaniment on the keyboard when she took her last breath.

She looked like an angel. At peace. And eventually, so were we. Eventually, peace does come to those who are left behind. And joy gradually flows in to fill the well of sorrow. I take great comfort in that knowledge.

And I hope you will take comfort from the beautiful stories in *A Cup of Comfort*® *for the Grieving Heart*.

—*Colleen Sell*

Hope

Our holidays of 1990 were a time of anticipation and wonder. Snow had fallen in late November, a rare occurrence in Seattle. We were greedy for more snowflakes as I wearied our children with stories of white Christmases when I was growing up in Michigan. Though the cold weather meant hand-carrying water from the house to the horses, cows, and chickens, it also meant snow forts, tracking coyote trails, and nighttime walks through the still woods. My husband Mark took our two children to sled on the hills of the west pasture. Even I, eight months pregnant, risked a few journeys down into the valley below. At the end of my long ride down, I would roll off the sled, beached in the high snow and laughing as our children, Brendan and Sara, tumbled down beside me.

Our baby was due after the holidays, and Christmas seemed even more touched with magic than ever. This was to be our last infant born to us; afterward, we planned to expand our family by adopting. Eventually, if we could manage it, we wanted six or seven children. We began the adventure to adoption while I was still pregnant with our third child. Mark and I filled out forms and questionnaires from our agency while resting beneath the Christmas tree. There was no hurry to adopt; it would take at least a year. Better, though, we decided, to get the papers in before the tumult and excitement of a new baby. We sent all our information off, knowing it would be a long time before we heard more.

With the holidays behind us, we busied ourselves making space in Sara's room for the new baby. Brendan pleaded for us to put the crib in his room, but he, at age seven, needed his sleep before facing a school day. Nonetheless, Brendan insisted on making part of his room baby-proof. He arranged his stuffed animals in a small circle, stapled a bright picture of ducks and chicks to his wall, and hung his old baby mobile above. This, he told me solemnly, was where he would watch the baby so I could take naps with Sara.

"No. I'll be watching the baby," Sara reminded Brendan. "After all, the baby is sleeping in my room."

Our three-year-old was thrilled with the superiority of her position.

Daniel Robinson Levy was born on a cold, gray day in late winter. Brendan and Sara competed to hold him and never tired of him. Brendan, in particular, would hold a sleeping Danny on his lap for hours, grinning down at his new brother. Sara would comb Danny's crazy shock of red hair while Brendan held Danny's small hands and clapped them gently together in rhythm to some made-up song. Danny smiled so early; at mere weeks old, he was grinning at the world. Surrounded by so much attention and love, who would not?

Spring arrived with hard rain and rough wind. When the sun would at last break through, the children and I would escape the house to work the gardens. While Brendan and I planted tall telephone peas, black-seeded Simpson lettuce, and Easter egg radishes into the cool soil of early spring, Sara bounced Danny in his carriage. Danny, bundled against the cold, kicked and chortled whenever we loomed over him and planted kisses on his rosy cheeks.

Like his siblings before him, Danny, too, was a night owl. Mark would get up with a groan and change the baby, then hand him off to me. Danny would nurse, coo happily to himself, and nurse some more. In the morning, Brendan would sneak into bed as well, gazing with pride at his little brother, who had at last drifted off to sleep with the dawn. Then Sara would wander in and crawl under the covers beside me. Mark would appear last, looking as weary as I felt. No matter the lack of sleep, the five of us would rest together, a small boat of happiness, sailing on life's seas.

When both Mark and I worked, all three children were often at my parents' house just down the lane. Even there, Sara and Brendan did not compete against their baby brother for attention; they held him and regaled Grandma with tales of his baby feats. "He knows my name," Sara reported. "He just can't say it yet."

When Danny would sit and stare out the window in those quiet moments before sleep claimed him, Brendan would interpret to his grandfather. "He likes to look out windows," Brendan solemnly intoned, as though this made Danny a small genius. Perhaps he was.

Summer in Seattle is an uncertain proposition, at best. Brendan's birthday, June thirteenth, dawned chill and damp. Danny had quieted about four in the morning, and I crept softly about in order not to wake him.

Before going to bed the night before, Mark and I had decorated the kitchen for Brendan's birthday, and the gay crepe banners clashed with the gray sky outside. Sara hopped about the room singing "Happy Birthday" while Brendan was served his breakfast in a manner befitting a king: pancakes on fancy china, crystal wine glass of orange juice, and bright cloth napkins. Oh, how Brendan was puffed up with happiness. School was over in a week, and Brendan's birthday party was going to be this weekend—only four days away!

"Give Danny a kiss for me," Brendan whispered as he raced off to the bus with Mark. "Tell him we're having birthday cake tonight."

That tableau is frozen forever in my mind. It was the last moment I ever felt pure happiness.

When Danny did not wake up that morning, I crept in to his and Sara's room and lay my hand on his little back. He was stiff and cold. He was dead. I knew immediately he had died of SIDS sometime during the night.

I cannot explain how, in a moment, life can go from blessed and joyous to complete wrenching horror. I stood rooted to the ground, faint and chilled. I had a crazy thought that I could magically turn time back, for just a night and a day. Could go back and rush in at his first cry of the evening before, could lift Danny and carry him through time to safety. Schooled to artificial calm through so many years of doctoring, I could not force tears even at this nightmare beyond words. I had a brief impression that in movies, when such a terrible scene occurs, the woman always shrieks. I opened my mouth and screamed. My houseguests raced upstairs at the sound.

"He's dead." I told them. "Danny's dead."

None believed me until they, too, touched his form. But I had already hurried downstairs, to find Sara and hold her. Sara, too, found this impossible. Our sweet baby could not be dead. She demanded to see him, and so we took Sara up to see, with her own wet eyes, the beloved brother lying still and rigid in his little crib. I called the police and the ambulance, my actions as stiff and frozen as my little boy, Danny, who lay upstairs.

Mark staggered in, and at last, I let myself cry— guilty tears, "if only" tears, tears of despair. The sheriff came next; a death outside the hospital must be investigated to ensure no foul play was involved. I never even saw the sheriff's face. My sobs racked me and I could not lift my face off Mark's lap as the sheriff spoke soothing words of useless, kind phrases. The sheriff's boots, gray alligator with a silver tip, are all I saw.

Then, the school day was over, and who would meet Brendan at the bus stop? Brendan, on his birthday; Brendan, waiting to come home and kiss his baby brother.

Mark did the hard task. Father and son walked down the long lane together. Brendan thought it a bad joke at first. Mark was a practical joker; surely, Brendan told me later, this was some terrible joke.

Sara met them at the door, struggling with such strange goings on, so much crying from her parents. "Emergency!" she announced to Brendan as she opened the front door. "Emergency! The baby's dead."

What can I tell you about grief? Such words are beyond me. A day passes and then another. That is the only truth I know. Worse, still, if such a thing is possible, was the suffering of our surviving children.

Anger is part of grief. I was bitter at anyone who had not lost a child, anyone who had not suffered. How could people work or eat or laugh? I have learned grief is ugly. I was irritable, unreasonable, and, at times, impossible. Going through grief takes such enormous sums of energy, there is nothing left over. Mark handled his grief by throwing himself into work. Brendan woke up each night and checked on all of us to make sure we were there, safe and breathing. I was like a wild animal in a small cage, pacing and fretting. In my agony, I was given to fits of restlessness and long walks. Sara, direct as usual, approached her grief by asking strangers for their baby. In grocery stores, I still hear her calling. "Hey, lady, our baby is dead. Can we have yours?"

That bitter summer passed. The children were still anxious and afraid to be away from me for even an hour or two. They knew death could strike anyone; death was not just for the old but for the young as well. I talked to them as we pulled the onions and carrots from the ground, as we harvested apples from the laden trees. Gradually, very gradually, they began to relax. Brendan and Sara had the gift of children. They could talk of grief, then they could put it away for a time. They laughed and chased each other in the orchard. What a balm it was to hear them, but what a sorrow too. Danny should be here as well, crawling through the tall grass, pulling himself up by the rough bark of a tree.

It was time for Brendan to start back to school. We had pulled him out those last few school days in June, after his birthday, after Danny' death. Now, school was hard for him, at first. Teachers and friends who had not heard the sad news asked after Danny, and I helped Brendan learn how to answer and to get through those first tough days.

We managed. We even, in spite of ourselves, got better. Not a day went by when I didn't think of Danny, but I began to smile again—though, always,

I thought, *Look, I'm not thinking about Danny.* There was nowhere to run from sadness, nor was there the desire to run from it—not if escape meant forgetting about Danny.

Autumn came with the tall trees lamenting their dead leaves. And we began to think of our old plans for a large family. Our courage had been drained by grief. Were we tempting fate to hope for more happiness?

An unexpected phone call forced us to make a choice. Our adoption agency, World Association for Parents and Children, called us with a surprise. An agency they were linked with wanted to work with us. There was a baby girl. Were we interested?

Our adoption social worker came out to the house several times to meet with us. Surprisingly, she did not think we were crazy to adopt six months after losing Danny. She worked with us. Our hearts opened up; we found the nerve to look forward. Humor has always been a salvation, and more and more, laughter kept creeping into our lives. Brendan and Sara had long ago returned to hilarity. Karen, our social worker, saw this as a mark of healing. Finally, we took a deep breath and nodded yes. Karen agreed.

Our second daughter was born in Georgia. Her birth mother had made an adoption plan, and our family was a good fit. Our agency continued to support us with classes and counseling. The only question became, "When?"

November arrived with powerful storms; we were often without electricity. Brendan and Sara loved when the lights went out; it meant hours in front of the fire talking to Mom or Dad, songs, and long nights huddled together in sleeping bags and under piles of blankets. We lost power three times that month, once for three days straight. Those nights always caused Brendan to ponder, to worry about Danny in the cold, dark ground, away from his family.

"We could," Sara would raise a chubby index finger, "take him some blankets." She looked at me. "I mean the ones we don't care about getting dirty."

I am sorry, but this is how children handle grief, how we should handle grief. We talked. Talk would turn to the new baby.

"Will she love us?" Brendan asked. "Will she let me hold her like I did Danny?"

Sara, my child of brutal honesty, wondered, "Will she die like Danny?"

We all wondered. Nevertheless, we all felt that seed of love growing toward a little girl we hadn't even met. We felt excitement and a strange budding joy. We felt hope.

At Thanksgiving, we argued about names for our little girl. We looked around the table and saw those who still lived, still laughed, still loved. Our grief was not less, but despair had been beaten back a while. There were tears around the table but also a new name: Emma Rose.

As Christmas approached, we set up two Christmas trees. One, a tall noble fir from the western meadow, sat in splendor in the living room. The other, a delicate hemlock, graced the playroom. We decked the fir with our usual hodgepodge of decorations, old family ornaments, popcorn strings, and bright construction paper chains. On Danny's tree, the gentle hemlock, we placed angels, tissue paper snowflakes, and paper messages of love. Sara could not write yet; she made drawing after drawing of baby Danny, crooked hearts, and smiling big sisters. Brendan wrote secret messages to Danny, tied them tightly with ribbon, and bound them to the tree. Like a Tibetan prayer wheel, Brendan spun the messages every time he walked by the tree. Each of us had a good cry under that tree, sometimes alone, sometimes on each other's shoulders.

We had much happiness as well. Emma Rose was coming soon and we had to prepare for her. New soft sheets and a bright yellow quilt Sara had picked out graced the old crib. I would often find Sara in her room, gazing into the empty crib, a quiet smile on her face.

"I miss Danny," she told me one morning. "But I want to give the new baby loving."

There was no snow that December, and I was glad of it when we headed to the airport one midnight just before Christmas to meet our new daughter. Mark and I were quiet on the ride there and as we waited for the plane to touch down. I was terrified and elated at the same time. I experienced the same inner turmoil I have subsequently had each time we have adopted or given birth. *What in the world are we doing? What kind of parents will we be? Is it too late to run away?* I now know such thoughts are laughable, but at that late moment in that quiet airport, I was frightened. Looking over at my husband's face, I could see similar feelings chase across his features.

In a moment's time, it seemed, the plane was there and a beautiful baby lay in my arms. Emma Rose's escort pleaded exhaustion at such a late hour and headed off to a hotel in preparation for leaving early the next morning. Other weary travelers scurried by until the airport felt abandoned by all but us three. It was a moment of enchantment; I was almost afraid to breathe for fear of breaking the spell.

Three-month-old Emma Rose had a big toothless grin and fat dimpled cheeks. Her little fingers grabbed my thumb and held on tight. With my other hand, I touched her soft, curly, dark hair. Here was our new daughter. Both Mark and I stood there with our jaws hanging open and goofy grins on our face. An older woman walked toward us; I heard her heels clicking noisily on the linoleum floor.

She paused and peeked down at our baby. "Isn't she the cutest thing?" She looked at both Mark and me. "She looks like a little Christmas angel, doesn't she?"

I could only nod mutely.

As we drove through the dark night to home, I sat in the back with Emma Rose, safely snuggled into a bulky car seat. She was still holding my finger, and her big brown eyes were looking everywhere. Mark had turned on the radio to lull her to sleep, and Christmas carols were playing. I sang along softly to "Silent Night" and felt close to tears with the power of the evening's events. As I sang, Emma Rose cocked her head toward me and squinted, her lips pursed together, and I halted, certain she was about to cry. Why wouldn't she? Here she was, coming across the whole country into the arms of strangers, driven through the dark night. Where was the foster mother she knew? Where were the familiar sights and sounds of her foster home? Then, suddenly, she opened her mouth wide and began to laugh. After a moment's startle, Mark and I joined in—three crazy people driving through the night, chortling. In that moment, on that dark, December road, we claimed our daughter and she claimed us.

Brendan and Sara met their sister the next morning. Emma Rose squealed, kicked, and yanked on their hair. They both fell promptly in love with her.

On Christmas morning, Brendan supervised Sara as they opened their presents. "Open them slowly," he cautioned her. "Mom and Dad like to watch us."

Emma was hurling fistfuls of bright wrapping paper into the air and laughing. She was not yet able to roll over and kept craning her head around to watch the other two children. Brendan kept repositioning her so she could keep an eye on the action. He tickled her tummy each time, sending her into new paroxysms of chuckles.

Emma Rose was wiggling so vigorously that she popped herself in the eye. Her whole face crumbled in shock and she burst into loud wails. I grabbed her up to comfort her, and she gradually subsided into soft whimpers.

Sara ran over to give the baby kisses, which somehow only infuriated Emma Rose more. Fresh howls filled the room.

Suddenly, Brendan was there holding an ill-wrapped present. He held it out, asking, "Should I open it for her?"

Emma quieted at the distraction and watched him intently. He carefully opened the package and handed her a soft white blanket—Danny's old blanket. "So she knows him," Brendan explained at my questioning gaze. "Because she might not remember him like we do."

"Hey," Sara had wandered over. "That was Danny's." She touched Brendan's back. "You are a smart big boy," she complimented him.

The blanket was already in Emma Rose's mouth and her usual grin had returned. Emma had a pile of new presents as well, but none have remained with her like that old worn blanket. It rests on her bed today.

Emma Rose is now twelve and a big sister herself four times over. Her laugh has never changed, nor has our love for her. She often pauses on the stairs to look over the many pictures of her brothers and sisters hanging there. Sometimes, I catch her touching Danny's picture, the one where he is gazing out from his little chair, his red hair standing straight up like Skeezix, and a sweet grin on his face.

"Hey, big brother," I've heard Emma Rose whisper. "I miss you."

Although Emma, like five of her siblings, has never met Danny, he will always be a part of their lives.

Brendan is a man now, as gentle and thoughtful as he was during those difficult days. He is also the kindest big brother I have ever known. Sara, almost a young woman, remains as truthful and forthright as she was as a little girl.

Danny's life will always be a treasure in my heart; his death will always be a most hard and bitter grief. Yet, Emma Rose's arrival that Christmas many years ago was an offering beyond measure. That holiday season saw tears and sadness but also healing and hope. There can be no greater gift.

—Marybeth Lambe

A version of this story was first published in Good Housekeeping *magazine, June 2004.*

Some Small Joy

Sometimes, amidst sorrow and despair, comes an unexpected blessing that is so beautiful it must be shared. Such a blessing is my husband Gerry's "Joy Book."

This daily journal came about during one of the worst times of Gerry's bout with esophageal cancer. He had dealt with radiation, chemo, extremely complicated surgery through his chest and his back, and the many horrific side effects from those procedures. Still, the wicked cancer would not leave his body.

Normally robust and fit, Gerry ran marathons as a young man and skied and played racquetball regularly as he grew older. Happy and outgoing by nature, he had an alter ego, a clown named Snappy, who, along with our daughter Robin, as Sweet Patootie, cavorted in parades and rest homes. Completely at ease in any kind of company, Gerry had the flair and quick thinking of a comedian, the eye of a photographer (which he was), and a constant, lively curiosity about the people and the world around him. He had a knack for getting the most out of every moment, for living "in the now," which was his motto.

Gerry possessed a certain *joie de vivre*—a joy of life—that drew me to him and kept me there for thirty-five years, until death took him from me. This and his many other qualities gave me some of the greatest moments of my life. We counted ourselves fortunate that our life together was filled with traveling from our California home to every state in the union, a wide and satisfying variety of interests, our ten wonderful children and their families, many different circles of friends, and a new adventure around every corner.

About eight or nine months into his cancer treatment, Gerry began to show signs of depression, anger, and bitterness, so unlike him. Such a reaction is, of course, perfectly normal and hardly unusual for those in his position, but for those of us who loved him, it was heartbreaking to see. He was especially agitated at bedtime, and so the process of preparing him for the night became tearful and anxious for both of us. Our oncologist (I say "our" rather than "his," as if cancer had happened to me as well, which, in a way, I suppose it did) encouraged Gerry to find some small joy in every single day. Dr. Sadar said that Gerry, of all people, with his characteristically positive outlook, knew well the value of laughter and joy. With his arm around my shoulders, the doctor said Gerry would want his family to remember those joys, rather than the anger and bitterness, for the rest of our lives. Cancer, he said, thrives on negativity and flees in the face of joy. This wonderful doctor, who had grown to admire Gerry, looked into his eyes and asked him to think about his suggestion to find joy in every day, for the sake of all of us.

Gerry got it. That blessed moment of joy in the throes of sorrow came the very next morning. When he opened his eyes, he looked at me, smiled, and said, "It's a joy to see your face in the morning." I laughed out loud, because I saw the old familiar twinkle in his blue eyes and heard that teasing, "Gerry-ness" in his voice. Truly, overnight, it was like getting him back.

We laughed together, and then he said thoughtfully, tongue-in-cheek, that it would give him great joy to go to Taco Bell for lunch. Taco Bell! I was much surprised, for he was eating almost nothing by then. But Taco Bell it was. As we sat at the little table eating burritos, it occurred to me that I had not seen him that happy for a long time. I will never forget his face, thin and pale but smiling, as he munched his joyous fast-food lunch.

When that was done, he said, "I think it would give me great joy to have something decadent for dessert. Like chocolate. A lot of chocolate!" So we got back in the car, no small thing for him because of his weakness and the tubes and blankets, and went to the wonderful chocolate store on Main Street downtown in our little mountain town of Grass Valley. There, he spent nearly half an hour carefully picking and choosing one chocolate piece after another, filling a bag with them, intently asking the clerk about each flavor. We walked across the street and sat on a bench, with Gerry wrapped in a blanket against the fall chill, and ate every piece of that decadent chocolate. He joked and laughed and commented on everyone who walked by, tourists and locals alike. Then, he asked me to go over and get some pasties (succulent little meat pies) for dinner. Pasties! For this man who could barely tolerate his favorite, rice pudding!

When I returned with the pasties, Gerry asked to go for a ride to see the fall leaves. Although he was tiring by then, he was not yet ready to end his day of joy. So we got back in the car, and I drove us through every street and back road I could think of where the leaves were turning. Gerry was from Boston, and our frequent trips to New England had been so special to us. We used to joke that, sure, Grass Valley has some pretty fall leaves, but it's no Foxboro, Massachusetts! But this drive was special, too. We saw Grass Valley with new, appreciative eyes, and those leaves truly were the finest we had ever seen. When, at last, we knew that he had to rest, we turned toward home, our hearts filled with joy.

From that day forward, the depression and bitter anger left Gerry completely. He also started his Joy Book.

Our daughter Kathy had given him a journal some months before, hoping he would write a daily record for her to cherish in his absence, but he could not bring himself to record those painful days. But when I brought out the journal after his emotional turn-around, he began to write in it daily. He wrote about his visitors and phone calls, about going out for lunch or a ride, about hugs and help from family, and, most precious to me, about having me with him. In his Joy Book, he captured small moments, like son-in-law Keith taking out the garbage: "*I find a lot of joy in that!*"

He also detailed introspective bursts of understanding: "*What a revelation I had today! Myrna was visibly upset because I went to the bathroom by myself, got dressed and did my toiletry all by myself without telling her, as promised, as I stood a good chance of falling again . . . a light went on in my head . . . I was ready to retaliate when I realized that's what I do when confronted with anger. Right away I stopped my aggressive behavior and a calm came over me . . . and when I hugged Myrna she too felt a calm. A revelation and a moment of joy!"* On another day, he wrote: *"Gave blood at Sierra Hospital. Did not use the wheelchair—JOY!"*

Sometimes he wrote something good he had for lunch or changes in his treatment: *"Best news of the day, Robin will be able to give me IV at home! Such Joy shared each day."*

We have a large, wonderful family, including thirty-seven grandchildren and great-grandchildren, who, thankfully, visit often. One day, when we had an unusually large number of kids and grandkids visiting, he listed all their names and then wrote, *"They all brought joy. In a bedlam sort of way."*

Before Gerry became ill, we often spent our New Year's Eves in unusual places when we traveled. That last year, we chalked one up to visiting the ER. Gerry wrote, *"Had to get X-rays last night and the nurse went 100 mph to get me back in time for New Year's."* (He'd meant to get him back to the ER room, where I was waiting for him.) *"I got there one minute before midnight and got a big kiss and hug and a Happy New Year. JOY!"*

During this same period, Gerry asked me to sit and talk with him for fifteen minutes at the end of every day, after he was in bed. "Fifteen minutes every single night," he said. "I want to talk about everything."

And so we did. Then he wrote about our conversations in his Joy Book. He wrote about daughter

Pam coming to watch football, losing five dollars to son Steve in a sports bet. And he wrote:

"Went to lunch with John, LaVell, and Art . . . we discussed this Joy Book and how it has helped my depression. I think the Joy Book has helped Myrna, too."

"Sat on the porch for an hour in the sun. Joy!"

"Kelly came and made chili and potato soup. What a joy!"

"Ron brought me a new heat blanket so I had two on that day, great joy!"

"Kelsey came by to say hello. Joy!"

"I fell just as Robin came in the door, she got me up with ease, that was joyful!"

"Got new insight today, thought Myrna and I as one person, not two."

"Marisa skated in a race and won all four. She was so elated I had to put it in my Joy Book."

I didn't read his entries in the Joy Book unless he asked me to, for they were his personal joys, though he would often show me. Later on, when he was unable to write them himself, he dictated and I wrote—but he always wanted to write the "Joy!" at the bottom himself. Some days he didn't want to write anything, unable to find joy in that particular day. But those days, to me, were the most important ones of all in which to find joy. So I encouraged him to dig a little deeper, and then he would write that he wasn't feeling sick that day or that they "Got blood in just one poke! Joy!"

He wanted everyone to have their own Joy Book. He wanted to spread the word about how much it helped, what comfort it gave him every evening, propped up on his pillows, reliving the joyful moments of each day. Yes, every single day, even if he had to hunt for it, he always found at least some small joy, and he managed to associate joy with every single person in our big family, so that each of their names are in the Joy Book someplace. Gerry's Joy Book enabled him to see firsthand how much he was loved, how much goodness there was in his life and in the world, and how much he had to offer us all. There is a fine, beautiful joy in that.

Gerry asked me to write about his funeral in that book and to write my own joys in it when I was alone. Even with his example before me, I struggle to find joy in each day without him. But I try. And you know what? It works. There truly is joy to be found in every single day. To me, however, it will always be found in Gerry's Joy Book. It was his comfort and now it is mine, and it is his gift to us. It has become both my treasure and my solace, a small joy in my life without him.

—Myrna Courtney

More Than a Dream

The room was made of light. White light. Blindingly bright and, at the same time, a balm for my eyes. If it were a room. There were no walls that I could see. No ceiling or floor. It was neither cold nor hot nor breezy. There were no smells in the air. If there was air. My mother was sitting across from me. Or beside me. Or inside me. It was hard to tell.

I knew I was asleep and dreaming, but it didn't matter. We were talking. Talking, talking, talking. We'd never been much for talking. Had always been good at yelling. Accusing. Blaming. And not speaking. But there we were. With no distractions. Talking from the heart. Or from the solar plexus. Maybe with the solar plexus. It's possible that no words were actually spoken out loud. Yet, we each knew exactly what the other was saying.

She told me about the day I was born. How angry she'd been with my father for choosing that day, that time, to take the car apart. Their only car. She was ready, I was ready, but the car was not. So she'd waited. Held the baby inside her, the last baby she'd ever have, the baby that was an afterthought, an accident, the baby that was me. Yes, you really were an accident. And she was sorry she'd ever told me that.

I noticed then the glow in her cheeks, the look of vibrant health. It surprised me, but I couldn't remember why. I told her that, even in high school, I'd cried on the mornings I had to go to school and she was home. It wasn't often that she was home. Her job was demanding. Menial but demanding. More so because of the odd hours, the irregular days, the time-and-a-half they paid for anyone willing to work on holidays. And her absence left a hole. It wasn't my intention to be cruel. I thought she should know. She said it hurt her, too. Leaving me every day. That was something I'd never considered.

The light was glowing brighter now. Inside me. Inside her. I saw that we were floating. It wasn't a surprise. It was a dream, after all.

I told her I hadn't always been a good girl. But I'd never been as bad as she'd always thought I was. I think she winced. It seemed to be out of my control— what I said and how I said it. Truth was flowing like a waterfall. Cleansing to the bone. Bone white. I imag- ined that light bleaching us to purity like old bones in the desert. I told her there was a very simple reason why she couldn't find tracks on my arms. There were none. Never had been. Not even one.

She sighed and shook her head. Said she knew that. She'd known that even before she looked. But she'd had to look. She said that sometimes a force took hold of her, took control and made her do things she knew were wrong. It was dark and powerful, got into her skin, her blood, her brain. It was the devil himself. She was afraid he'd have me, too. I told her that sometimes he did. She said, I know.

I told her then about the time my friends and I had stolen a flashing caution light and placed it on the front lawn of a boy we knew. The boy whose father was our history teacher. It was a bad choice. We'd not been as clandestine as we thought. Hadn't noticed the streetlamp illuminating the license plate of our car. They had a friend who worked at DMV. We were very nearly suspended from high school. I think she almost smiled.

I went on to bigger things—boyfriends. Confirmed her greatest fear—that her youngest daughter, while still very young and unmarried, had not been a virgin. I told her about needing to feel that someone knew I was alive. Needing to be touched. She'd never cared much for touching. She dropped her head. She hadn't always been that way and she wanted me to understand, but she knew that understanding was not excusing. She told me she'd shrunk away from human contact as a girl. Went on to explain, but I wasn't listening to what she said. I was hearing what she didn't say. She didn't say I was bad. Didn't say she was disgusted with me. Didn't throw me away.

I said, I wonder why it is that mothers and daughters can't get along. She said, Maybe you'll make it different. I sighed. She'd been bugging me for years: When are you going to have a baby? I want grandchildren.

I'd always reminded her that she already had grandchildren. Lots of them. She always said, "I want your grandchildren."

I looked again at her glowing cheeks. Saw that it was fever. Not health. She was fading, and we hadn't discussed the most important thing. I cleared my throat. She spoke.

I wish you hadn't waited so long. Her eyes drifted down to my belly. Nothing was showing yet.

I wish you'd never smoked. It was a wish I'd always held. I tried not to sound accusing. Tried not to think about the years of respiratory infections, the colds and pneumonias and lengthy absences from school.

I won't even know if it's a boy or a girl. She sounded matter of fact. No, you won't. It's not fair. But it's not my fault you won't be here. Life is seldom fair. I had two days. Two days to enjoy the thrill of expecting your baby before they told me I'd never see your baby. We all get our just desserts. Mine is cancer.

Two days. We'd actually planned to wait a little longer. Not much. A couple more months. Then I'd had that flash. A sudden urgency. A voice that told me, Now. Or she'll never know. I'd told her about my pregnancy as soon as I found out. The only person I'd told first was my husband. Two days later, they told her the cancer had spread to her brain. They gave her six weeks, tops. Two days. I'd had one. One day of feeling my feet firmly planted on this planet. One day of being so acutely alive I could feel the breeze rustling every single hair on my head, could taste the sunlight. It was the day I found the old calendar page she'd saved, the page with a notation: Mary lost her first tooth today. I didn't tell her, but she heard me anyway. I felt her eyes welling.

It's going to be a home birth, Mom. I hadn't planned to tell her that. I braced myself for an argument.

She raised an eyebrow.

I said, I've had enough of hospitals.

She nodded. Will it be safe?

It will be safe. It was the inevitable question. Why did people assume I would be careless? I felt myself becoming defensive. Sensed our talk coming to an end. I have a good doctor. He's done this many times.

I trust your judgment.

What did she say? I'd waited a lifetime to hear those words. An entire lifetime. I tried not to look shocked. We were running out of time.

I love you, Mom.

I love you, too.

The light was beginning to dim. Her face becoming indistinct. I opened my eyes to a bright summer morning. The conversation still blazed in my head. Filling me.

I showered, dressed, hurried to the hospital.

She was sleeping peacefully. I sat and waited and watched. I'd been worried what all of this was doing to my unborn child. All the time inside hospitals, doctors' offices. All the bad news and pain. Watching my mother deteriorate.

I noticed that the hospital air was less stifling that morning.

My mother opened her eyes and smiled. "You're still here."

"I just got here."

She wasn't fully awake yet. I offered her a drink of water. She accepted it, then looked at me, studied my face. "You were here all night. We talked and talked and talked."

—Mary Rudy

Gifts

The news stories predict a huge party, balloons rising, the ball dropping, the new year rolling in at midnight with kisses, champagne, and a shared sense of hope and possibility. I sit quietly, as if being very still will suspend time. On this cold morning of December 31, the sky outside is dark, too early for the Minnesota winter sun to attempt an appearance. I sit at the same kitchen table where we used to sit together eating Cap'n Crunch. As the kitchen fills with the smells of French roast coffee and toasted wheat bread, I allow myself to remember. The years dissolve into my own heartbeat, and I recall another New Year's Eve, twenty years ago, when I was still dressed in party clothes as I claimed his, no longer needed . . .

As I brushed on gold eye shadow that sparkled and swept my still naturally blond hair into a French twist, I was struck by the passing of time. I had been alive for thirty-three New Year's Eves. How the hell had that happened? I could already see distinct lines forming around my eyes.

The jangling phone pulled me from my thoughts. I caught it just before the answering machine kicked in.

"Is this Josh's mother?"

A sense of trepidation washed over me. "It is. Who am I speaking to?"

"This is Max from the Bloomington Skate Park. Your son—he fainted or something; he isn't conscious. The EMTs are working on him."

Working on him? Not conscious? What?

"No, no, no-no-no-no," I told the voice on the phone, "I just saw him a few hours ago; he was fine. Are you absolutely sure it's my Josh?"

"His friend Zack was with him; he gave me your number."

"My husband already left to pick up the boys. Is he there?"

"Zack said he's not here yet, but when he gets here, I'll tell him you're on your way to the hospital. Yes? They're taking your son to Burnsville Ridges."

Burnsville Ridges was easily a half-hour away. Jeff had taken my car, which left his with its manual transmission. I'd never driven a stick-shift, and it probably wasn't the time to learn, panicked and in rush-hour traffic. I called my father-in-law, who lived within fifteen minutes, ten when I was at the wheel. I paced while I waited the eternity it took for Martin to get to my house. If his car were an automatic, I'd have driven us to the hospital. Instead, I had to hold my stomach tight so I wouldn't scream at him to hurry the hell up . . . so I wouldn't scream, period. My mind kept replaying the voice on the phone as distressing questions raced through my mind. *How long had Josh been unconscious? Was he breathing?*

Neither Martin nor I knew Burnsville. We got turned around and got lost, again and again, as evening fell and the holiday officially began. It took us an intolerably long time to find the suburban hospital.

When we finally walked through the emergency entrance, we found my husband Jeff sitting alone in the empty waiting room. At 6 feet, 2 inches tall, he somehow looked very small, and I noticed a stoop to his normally erect shoulders. His jaw was tightly set, and I could tell he was having a hard time meeting my eyes. My stomach flipped and my throat tightened. He is braced for the worst, I knew. *Oh, my god, what was the worst? How long had he been sitting like that all by himself?*

The doctor appeared and, taking my hand, he said. "Is that your little boy we just had in the ER?"

It registered at some level within me that the weary look on the doctor's face wasn't good. But it mattered so much to me that the doctor understood that, even at age fourteen and over six feet tall, Josh was still my very little boy. I whispered "yes," but no sound came out. The doctor read my lips and squeezed my hand firmly.

"We couldn't stabilize your son's heart. Your husband asked for a cardiac surgeon, so an ambulance took him to Hennepin County Medical Center."

On the way to Hennepin, I learned that the attending physician had asked Jeff if he wanted a priest. They must have known then that there was no hope. As my husband related that conversation, I imagined him telling the doctors in his quiet but very serious you-*will*-listen-to-me tone that he didn't want a priest for his son, he wanted a surgeon.

By the time we got downtown, Josh was gone. It was too late for a surgeon, probably from the time he'd collapsed. His heart rhythms refused to stabilize. We would come to learn decades later that he died of sudden arrhythmia death syndrome (SADS), a genetic heart condition that can cause sudden death in young and seemingly healthy people.

We'll never know if Josh knew, if he had any warning or understanding, of what was happening to him. I'll never know if he was afraid. Or if he needed me. I'd carried him in my womb, birthed him, and held his head as he vomited whenever he had one of his migraines. I'd put him on the bus the first day of every school year, crying my way to work because every "first" felt so emotional and so important. I'd sat quietly with him when, at thirteen, he despairingly grieved the loss of his first, and as fate would have it, only love. All those moments, all those milestones, and it is still, all these years later, completely and utterly unthinkable that I wasn't there with him when he drew his last breath. It still feels almost intolerable that he and I shared no conscious connection that his very life, and mine as I knew it, was coming to an end.

The emergency room at Hennepin was so packed with sick and injured people that there were no rooms open. The nurse moved Josh's body to a small space that held supplies so we could have privacy. It was surreal to be in what was basically a supply closet with mops, pails, and racks of bandages, where Josh lay on the gurney, his beautiful blond hair tangled and his skater T-shirt torn open. His body was so long that his feet popped out from under the sheet.

I could just imagine Josh rolling his eyes, could almost see him wink at me. As Jeff and I each held one of his hands, I thought I felt his spirit leave. There seemed to be a shift in the air around us, like he had been in the room and then left. I like to imagine that his spirit was waiting so we could say goodbye, so he wouldn't have to leave the earth all by himself with no farewell. He never liked being alone. Sometimes, I just need to believe that he left with some sort of company.

We were home by 8:00 P.M. We'd been gone two hours. And we came home to lives completely changed, even as the shell of our world looked disturbingly the same. Our Christmas tree was still displayed, obscenely it seemed now, in the living room window, and the smell of Norway pine met us at the front door. Sparkling crystal icicles hung from the ceiling, catching the lights and flickering them across the room. I felt like throwing up when we walked into our holiday house, both it and we decorated for a different life, a life that was gone forever.

On the way home, we had picked up our younger son, Miles, from his overnight YMCA party, thinking he would never forgive us, or worse, never forgive himself, if he had played and laughed in ignorance of his brother's death. With our Toyota Camry idling in the frozen parking lot, the three of us sat in the backseat of the car as Jeff and I somehow told Miles that his only brother was gone. How do you explain that to an eight-year-old? How could he even understand? His pal, his conspirator, his coach, and at times his tormentor, was gone, just like that. I can't even remember what words we used to tell Miles that his favorite person in the whole world was dead.

That first horrible night, only one of many, we ended up bringing a futon into our bedroom so Miles could sleep close by. He would have been too far away and too lonely upstairs without his big brother. We held him until he finally drifted off, tears still wet on his cheeks.

I had already lived through some really hard times myself, and as a therapist I had supported people through horrendous losses. Maybe because of that, I knew even that first night that it would somehow get less painful to live without Josh. I knew time would soften the harsh line between before and after. Knew this and resented it. Knew it even as I clenched my nails into the palms of my hands to stop myself from screaming. We would find some way to go on without him, and I found that reprehensible.

Life goes on all around a grieving family, but within the grieving family, life doesn't just go on. Everything is different and difficult. Even breathing hurts. Minutes can seem like hours. And there are

thousands of firsts to get through: The first morning without him. The first weekend without him.
The first time driving past his school. The first time
seeing a skateboarder on the street. The first time
you realize your child's scent has left his pillowcase,
never to be replaced.

Only the gift of time dulls the pain inside and
restores some semblance of "normal" to your life. But
nothing is ever quite the same. And nothing ever
completely fills the void left in your heart.

In times of death, people give what they can.
Some people gave us food. Our frozen porch was
stacked with casseroles, pans of chicken wings, bowls
of mashed potatoes, and pots of soup—food that
emotionally nourished us even though most of it
never got eaten.

Our friends Jim and Therese came during the
night and set up fourteen luminaries leading up the
path to our front door. They came over every evening
for a week, setting up fresh paper-sacks and candles,
taking them away early in the morning. Somehow,
they guessed that seeing the burnt-out remnants of
the candles and the flattened, sodden bags would be
too brutal as we faced the morning. I sat and looked
out the window late at night, watching the candles
burning brightly, seemingly lighting the way back

home, just in case. Fourteen candles, one for each of Josh's years on the earth.

We also remember the people who moved into our lives after Josh's death because of the people who moved out. Their absence was palpable.

Most poignantly, though, we remember the people who moved in closer because we needed them and because, like many grieving people, we couldn't ask. I do understand why some people kept their distance, though. It's not easy staying close to grieving parents. We're sad, we feel guilty, and we're angry. Much of the time, we're inconsolable. During the early months, it takes real strength and courage to be connected to us, but we appreciate those who do, forever.

On January 4 we were readying ourselves for Josh's wake. The house was dark, deathly quiet, encased in grief. The falling snow outside was so brilliantly white it assaulted our senses, almost sickening in its beauty. Jeff and I lay in our bedroom with the lights off and the blinds drawn, trying to find some space to be that was less intolerable than all the spaces we'd tried. We weren't talking; we weren't even crying anymore.

My oldest sister, Steph, was in the dining room silently compiling pictures for the funeral. Stacks of photographs covered the mahogany table—images of Josh and Miles skateboarding, wrestling, playing football, baseball, basketball. A photo of Josh and Miles with our big woolly dog, Kashif, who they had dressed in a skater T-shirt.

While Steph worked, stopping only to refill her coffee cup and to blow her nose, Kashif lay quietly under the table. He had been subdued since smelling Josh's jacket that first night. He'd sat in front of the chair over which we had draped Josh's jacket, whimpering and crying. We didn't know what he smelled and we didn't know how he knew, but he hadn't been himself since. He barely acknowledged all the strangers who came and went. Poor puppy, he was a guard dog with nothing left to guard.

As Jeff and I lay quietly, each trapped in our own thoughts, we heard the doorbell chime. A minute later, Steph knocked on our bedroom door, informing us we had a visitor. We came out to find a distant relative of Jeff's. He was a huge man, dark-eyed, dark-skinned, and wearing a dark suit. His mass and energy filled our small living room. We didn't know him very well, but we knew he was a preacher. He had come to our house that afternoon because he had something to give.

He formed us into a small circle and began to pray. Kashif, who resembled a well-fed black-and-silver wolf, came running into the room. He sat down regally in the middle of the circle, periodically snuffling the crotch of the preacher man. In between snuffles, Kashif held his head impressively high, proud, sure all the fuss was for him.

As we all stood holding hands, heads bowed, our eyes would sneak peeks at Kashif. The preacher's deep velvety voice rose and fell with intense emotion and sincerity as he delivered the gift he brought us, his verbal casserole.

The sense of unreality that had been hovering for the past few days descended and enveloped me. I couldn't correct Kashif, couldn't do anything to stop him unless I broke the circle. I stealthily lifted a foot and pointed it in Kashif's direction. My warning went completely unheeded. My eyes moved between Kashif's insistent attentiveness to the preacher's crotch and the droplets of dirty snow that fell off the preacher's large dark shoes onto our pink-and-cream rug. I watched as the woven Danish tulips disappeared under the melting pool of slush. I knew I shouldn't care, even notice, but still I cringed as I watched the mess form.

I knew without looking that my sister was holding her breath. She was mortified by the dog's impertinence. And I knew she was worried I'd start to laugh—or worse, that she would. I looked at Jeff and met his eyes. They looked tired and red from crying, but they were dancing with recognition. He understood the silent sister-drama that was taking place. He knew that Steph and I were trying not to start laughing, and he knew that if we started, we wouldn't be able to stop, that we would end up hysterical and inappropriate. His knowing made it even harder to control myself.

The absurdity of the situation washed over all of us, except for the preacher. Our shoulders shook with the laughter we were holding in. There we stood, three disheveled agnostics, in a prayer circle, while this bigger-than-life, soap-and-water-smelling Baptist minister exalted our child's entry into heaven and the righteousness of the Lord for calling him home. He prayed for Josh's soul; he prayed for ours. He invited us to be saved. We declined.

The irony and the sheer energy of the moment were such contrasts to the past four days that we could barely contain ourselves. I managed to choke out a "Thank you" and to show the preacher to the door. As soon as the door closed, before he had even made it down the steps, we fell headlong into healing pools of laughter. We howled, we snorted, we cried. And then we howled some more. Kashif was confused but oh so happy that the house was no longer quiet. He leapt with excitement, running between us and jumping on us. Maybe he thought the worst was over.

We knew the worst hadn't even really begun, but for a few moments, the very essence of Josh was with us again—loud, rambunctious, irreverent, and exuberant. The feeling of his presence, his life energy, held our hearts and jumpstarted our brains. Now I could remember that Josh filled his days completely, drew notice every time he walked into a room, and always left behind a trace of himself.

We received a very different gift than the preacher thought he was bringing, one that was far better than we knew to ask for.

—*Lindsay Nielsen*

Gone Fishing

"I'm going fishing!" Dad announced from his in-home hospital bed. He was as excited as a little kid.

"Fishing?" I smiled, kissing his gray, scratchy cheek.

"Yeah! I can't wait to go."

As I gave my mother a quick peck on the cheek, too, we exchanged glances. Since Dad's latest stroke, his mind had wandered farther and farther from reality. Most of his strange thoughts and benign hallucinations were unbelievable or downright impossible. Still, they were quite real to him. Experience had taught me that it was best to just go along with whatever he said; it truly cut down on everyone's frustration levels, especially Dad's.

Yet, this particular episode had accomplished something none of the others had: It had improved his mood, really bucked him up. It was good to see him looking forward to something, anything. So, naturally, I played along with him while Mom took a much-needed out-of-the-house break.

I tried to interest Dad in some supper, but all he wanted was to talk about his upcoming trip. I only half listened to him babble on in his broken, stroke-impaired speech, until he mentioned a name.

"You mean Joe from down the street is taking you fishing?" I asked. This seemed unlikely, because this neighbor was the only Joe we knew and we scarcely knew him at all.

"No, not Joe. Jo, my Jo."

My heart skipped a beat. Although my folks had been married for more than twenty years and had raised a blended family together, they'd never claimed that theirs was a "love match." They'd both lost their soul mates thirty years before, and Dad's first wife, Jo, had been the true love of his life.

I took a deep breath to steady my foreboding. "What makes you think that Jo is going to take you fishing?" Dad rolled his eyes patiently while he patted my hand. "She came to visit."

"Visit?" I questioned, thinking dead people don't come for visits. "When?"

"Last night."

"Oh." Relief passed over me. "You dreamed about going fishing with Jo last night."

"No!" Dad shouted angrily, his eyebrows crinkled in agitation. "No. Jo came here. We're going fishing."

"Okay, okay. Don't get so upset," I placated him quickly. "When is she coming to take you fishing?"

"Three days!" he grinned triumphantly, holding up three fingers. "Monday!"

Suddenly, Dad ran out of steam, his energy zapped by his exuberant conversation. He sank back onto his pillow, waving aside his dinner completely. Two seconds later, he was fast asleep.

But I was wide awake. Carefully, I set his untouched dinner on his bedside table. Falling into a nearby rocking chair, I closed my eyes then rubbed them. Dad's "visit" with his long-dead wife filled me with dread. The doctor had warned us that Dad's time on this earth was drawing to a close. But to have my father talk so happily about seeing Jo again was completely unnerving. My insides clenched, as I grinded my teeth against my impending loss.

Ever since I could remember, Dad had taken me out to the cemetery on every holiday, most memorably on Jo's birthday. We'd pick up a fresh bouquet of colorful seasonal flowers—daisies in the spring, wildflowers in the summer, mums in the fall, poinsettias in the winter, roses anytime. The routine was always the same. First, he'd kiss Jo's headstone and ask her how she was doing. He'd always pause for a moment, as if he were genuinely listening to her answer. Then, he'd point to me and say to Jo, "Isn't she beautiful? Hasn't she grown? And she's smart as a whip."

Over the years, he'd "shown" her most of my report cards; even my diploma made a trip out to the cemetery. I had always been embarrassed by his boastful claims on my behalf and would blush, as if Jo were capable of enjoying my list of accomplishments. Of course, in Dad's eyes, Jo was. Dad would continue to "talk" with her as he tidied up her gravesite. Once all the weeds were pulled and he'd carefully arranged her flowers, Dad would reminisce to me about his Jo. Most of his stories were funny ones that had taken place during their wonderful fishing trips. Before we left, we'd always sing a version of "Happy Birthday to You" that was boisterous enough to wake the dead.

Later on, Dad and I would stop at our favorite restaurant to enjoy chocolate cake with caramel icing accompanied by a large scoop of vanilla ice cream. It was a fun outing that both of us looked forward to every year. Years later, after I was all grown up and Dad could no longer drive, we still managed to celebrate Jo's special day. Due to Dad's ill health, however, her last graveside birthday party had been somewhat different. I had planted the flowers while Dad sat in the car thoughtfully looking on. Afterward, we'd stopped at a small drive-through ice cream stand. Somehow, in my heart, I'd known this would be the last time Dad and I would enjoy this celebration together.

"Is it Monday?" Dad awakened from his nap. His question startled me.

"No, it's still Friday evening. Are you really that anxious to leave for your vacation?"

Dad smiled and then shrugged pensively. "Yeah. I'm tired." No doubt that was true. Dad had been sick for a long, miserable time, and he'd earned his rest.

"So are you going up to Canada to the cabin where you and Jo always stayed?"

"Oh, yeah!" His mind seemed to be racing while I supplied the words that fit his visions of his upcoming holiday.

"The smell of pine trees and wood smoke," I recalled for him. "That early-morning fog will bring the best fish to the worms. All you two will have to do is cast your lines into the water and wait for the trout to bite. Then Jo will slap a thick hunk of butter into the pan and fry those babies right up. A little coffee, a couple of honey buns, and breakfast is served!"

Dad grinned and smacked his lips hungrily.

"We'll have fun." He offered a confidential and playful wink. I laughed out loud. The picture of my dad, younger, stronger, and healthier than I'd ever known him, danced through my head. It was so easy to envision the two of them laughing and delighting in each other once more. Their reunion would be great for him but sad for me.

"I'll miss you, Daddy." I whispered quietly, holding back my tears.

He cupped my cheek, his eyes softening. He didn't talk, but his eyes spoke volumes.

"And you'll miss me too," I said, while he nodded. "But someday, we'll meet at that lake and have a huge party together!"

"Absolutely!" Dad agreed and then lay back down wearily. "Monday I'm going fishing."

"With Jo."

That's exactly what I hope happened the following Monday morning when my father took his last breath.

I've lost many other loved ones since then. After each passing, I always imagine all of them up at the lake with Jo and Dad, gossiping, laughing, happy to be fishing together again. And though I've raised two kids of my own and no longer live near that old cemetery with its weather-worn headstone and sunken markers, our family tradition continues. Every August 24, I bake a double-layer chocolate cake, scoop up globs of vanilla ice cream, and sing "Happy Birthday, Dear Daddy" to the sky.

—*Loy Michael Cerf*

So Soft Her Goodbye

Wallpaper! At last, this was to be the day. It was a beautiful, sunny afternoon in July, and we had been planning this outing for some time. The baby was in his carriage, my husband was ready, and I was looking forward to selecting wallpaper with a child-at-Christmas-like enthusiasm.

The phone rang. I ran to pick it up.

"I'm sick. Can you come over?" It was my grandmother. I don't recall her ever asking me for anything prior to this. Ever!

"Hurry," she continued. "I'm so sick."

"What's wrong? What do you mean 'sick'?"

"I don't know. I just feel sick."

"Where?" I pressed.

"I don't know. I just don't feel right."

"Where's Grandpa?" I asked.

"Right here," she answered. "Can you come?"

"Of course. I'll be right there."

"How long will you be?" she asked plaintively.

"Five minutes."

"Really? Only five minutes?"

"Yeah."

"You've always been there when I need you," she said.

I would have to ponder that one. I could only recall her being there when I needed her.

I ran past my husband. "Watch the baby. Something's wrong with my grandmother. I have to go right over there."

I vaguely remember my husband offering to go in my stead. He is a physician; I, only a granddaughter. Somehow, I knew the need for granddaughter overrode the need for doctor at that moment.

In the taxi on the way there, I felt an uneasiness that I couldn't attribute to my grandmother saying that she felt ill. After all, it might only have been a flu. But something else was niggling at me, something not quite tangible, something I couldn't yet pinpoint. Yet, it remained there, a vague, uneasy feeling, cloaked in an equally vague sense of fear.

I swept past the doorman, probably forgetting to say "hello." I rode the elevator to the sixth floor and raced to 6-E. So many years—that number was indelibly etched in my memory: 6-E. I rang the bell.

My grandfather answered, my grandmother standing about ten feet behind him. She looked frail and pale, despite the enviable thick, brown hair and the still trim, firm figure.

Grandma outstretched her arms to me. "Gladys," she cried. "Gladys. It's been so long." She ran toward me, crying and then embracing me.

But Gladys was my mother, her daughter, dead thirteen years. I said nothing, not daring to correct her. My grandfather stood, startled, shaking his head in disbelief, tears in his eyes.

Then, that feeling returned, inching its way through me. That odd, vague feeling, not attributable to the obvious question, of why she thought I was my mother. It was something else, something as-yet undefined behind that obvious question, that rattled me.

"What's wrong, Grandma?" I asked.

She looked at me for a minute, dazed and confused. "Wrong?"

"You said you felt really sick," I prompted.

"I'm okay now," she said. "I just feel so weak and tired. I don't know what was wrong."

Then, she called me by my name. I was back. She was back, apparently forgetting she had just mistaken me for her daughter.

"Let's talk," I suggested.

She led me into the living room, holding my hand, while my grandfather called the doctor. We chatted for a while, I don't remember about what. Not until she placed her hand gently on my face.

"You're so beautiful," she said. "I could look at you forever."

She put her arms around me, and we hugged. I could feel every bone in her body. *God, had she gotten that thin?* Then that feeling again, this time pushing its way—no, forcing its way—to the surface. It was coming into focus now. Her words. It was her words. Every word, every sentence seemed like a closure. I shook the thought from my mind.

My grandfather called me into their bedroom. The doctor attributed the episode to old age and declining health. Only weeks before, he had examined my grandmother and found nothing specifically wrong. His suggestion was to do nothing.

My grandfather whipped up some lunch for us. Afterward, we sat and talked for hours. When it felt safe for me to leave, I went home.

I was home for only about two hours when the phone rang again.

"Send Martin over! Quick!" This time it was my grandfather's voice, asking for my husband. He hung up on me before I could question him.

I went tearing through the house, screaming for my husband to race over to my grandparents'. He tore past me, slamming the door. After frantic efforts to find a neighbor to babysit and succeeding at last, I, too, ran out, shaking, afraid of what I'd find at 6-E.

To my relief and surprise, my grandmother opened the door. I was shocked to see that her lips, usually a soft pink, were now an alarming pale blue. I looked questioningly at my grandfather. He said nothing in her presence. However, when alone, he explained how, only moments earlier, he had found my grandmother slumped over her dinner plate. When he attempted to rouse her, she was unresponsive. He lifted her face to find her lips a sickening shade of dark blue. He had been sure she was dead.

He looked at me, tears pooling in his eyes. "I couldn't take it. I wasn't ready for her to go. Sixty-three years of marriage . . . " his voice trailed off.

After a moment, he continued: "So I took her and slapped her face. She still didn't move. Then I threw a glass of ice water at her." He looked amazed as he proceeded, "And she woke up. Just like that. Back from the dead. I was astonished."

Again, he paused, and his amazement faded to worry. "But her lips, they're still bluish. You saw them. And that other shade of blue, before she got some of the color back . . . " He shuddered.

"Shouldn't we take her to the doctor?"

"I called. The doctor said there's nothing he can do for her. It's not her heart; it's not a stroke. It's old age. Better she's at home," he said. "But those blue lips, what was that?" he asked rhetorically.

The blue lips. The blue lips. I had seen the blue lips of death once before. It looked nothing like this. I passed off the thought, leaving the room for my husband and grandfather to talk while I joined my grandmother in the dining room.

I made tea, and we sat together sipping from Grandma's antique china cups and nibbling on Fig Newtons—her favorite. It seemed odd for someone who had just "died" to be sitting there, less than an hour later, munching away so avidly on Fig Newtons. At the same time, it made me wish for more time with her, to savor every moment I had with her as she had always savored life.

I couldn't take my eyes off of my grandmother. I just sat, staring—half out of a desire to soak up every ounce of her and half out of fear she'd drop dead on the spot. Finally, I allowed my eyes, so tired from all that staring, to wander along the table. That's when I noticed the bottles: aspirin, vitamins, and bottles of my grandfather's prescription medications. *Time-release pills*, I thought. I suspected they were time-released because of the multicolored little pellets sifting inside each half-clear and half-blue capsule. Half-blue capsule! I straightened up, taking a closer look. Blue. Royal blue.

On a hunch, I opened the bottle and removed one of the tiny capsules. I looked, first at it, then at my grandmother's lips, which were, as she consumed more and more tea, regaining their original color. I dashed into the kitchen and ran the capsule under hot water until my fingertips absorbed some of the color from the capsule. I was flooded with indescribable relief and joy. But, to make sure my conclusion was accurate, I dashed back to the dining room to ask the requisite question.

"Grandma," I tried to sound casual, but was bursting. "Did you take any pills today?"

She nodded, as I expected her to do.

"Which pills?" I continued.

She pointed to the bottles on the table.

"Why?" I asked.

She looked impatient. "I told you," she said, "I don't feel well. I feel weak and tired, so I took some vitamins."

Vitamins. I pressed on, despite her obvious boredom with the topic. "Which bottle?" I waited, holding my breath.

"That one." She reached for the prescription bottle of blue capsules.

"How many did you take?" I asked.

"A few. I told you, I felt weak and I thought maybe some vitamins would help me."

I walked—no, ran—back to my grandparents' bedroom, holding up my royal blue fingertips. "Is this the color blue that Grandma's lips were?"

My grandfather looked shocked. "Yes. Exactly that color blue. I don't understand . . . " he said, puzzled.

I pulled out my other hand, holding the now-obvious culprit, the bottle of medication. At once, he understood. He put his hand to his mouth.

"She took your pills by mistake. She thought they were her vitamins."

My grandfather followed me to the dining room, where I showed him all the bottles sitting in front of my grandmother on the table. He placed his arms around her and then gently asked her to tell him what she had said to me moments before. He then explained to her what had happened. It seemed to register, as she was very quiet. He removed all his pills and put them high up in the kitchen cabinet.

My grandfather figured my grandmother must have taken enough pills, thinking they were vitamins, not only to color her lips but also to render her temporarily unconscious. He called her doctor. Whatever happened, the doctor offered, the crisis was over. We still had Grandma.

We stayed on for dinner, again to savor the moments this reprieve had offered. There was no thought of anything different; we all had to be together. And when we were confident the danger was over, I went home for my son and brought him back with me. The house took on the radiance of life as my grandparents played with their great-grandchild.

During a lull, my grandmother looked up at my grandfather. "I'm sorry for all the trouble I've been these last few years . . . " She said nothing more. There it was again. Another closure.

My grandfather walked over and held her. "You've never been trouble," he said. "Never. Not for a moment."

We went home, planning to meet the next day. We weren't stupid. It was becoming clear that we were being given some extra time. It was ours to use or not. We grabbed for it—whether out of fear or intuition or the stark realization that people don't last forever, I don't know. I only knew that I had to be with my grandmother the next day, that we all had to be with her. And we were. All five of us drove in the car and picked up some McDonald's fries, which my grandmother devoured. It made me feel good to watch her enjoying them. She chided my husband and me for "acting like babies" during a momentary skirmish we had in the car. That made me feel good, too. Grandma was back—the alert, sharp, funny (though she didn't know it) Grandma I knew and loved. But there was a "but." She continued to complain of feeling increasingly weak and tired—more than she had ever felt in her life. My antennae were up, poised.

The next day my grandmother was too weak to get out of bed. My aunt, her daughter, came in from Pennsylvania. Her other grandchildren, my cousins, came over, too. We all spent the day. This time, I left my son at home, once again unsure of what I'd find when I arrived at 6-E.

Grandma became increasingly worse as the day wore on. Then she stopped talking, too weak to even try. But, instead of sleeping, she became restless. Her housekeeper and longtime companion stood at the door of my grandparents' bedroom, teary-eyed, frantic at her inability to effect a positive change, despite her best efforts. We hired a private nurse, just in case.

Grandma continued to become increasingly more restless. She kept getting into bed only to get out a few minutes later. In and out, in and out, over and over again, until the nurse left the room in tears, muttering that my grandmother was using up her last stores of energy.

It was a physiological agitation. The doctor said that a tranquilizer, at that time, was contraindicated, as it could suppress her respiratory system and in so doing lead to death. He went on to say, however, that this type of physical agitation and restlessness sometimes precedes death. My grandmother's body, in essence, was short-circuiting. Her mind was working, but her body was failing and sending out signals of distress. It was torture to watch. She couldn't rest, couldn't talk, couldn't do anything but climb in and out of the bed, unable to find comfort in any position.

As the hours passed, I became increasingly nervous and upset, and I allowed an intruding thought to creep into my consciousness. I knew what I had to do. I just wasn't ready. But I'd never be ready. I knew that, too. Maybe this is what Grandma had been saying for days. Maybe we all knew it but didn't want to believe it, that this active, full-of-life, loyal-to-the-end, amazing woman could ever die. Surely, she would live forever. She'd be the first. She'd make history, all the medical journals, the *Guiness Book of World Records*. She would be the only person on Earth to live forever. Only Grandma seemed to know better.

"Someday this will be yours," she had said frequently in recent months. I didn't want to hear it. I didn't want any part of such talk. I didn't, after all, believe she'd ever die.

"Let me show you how to keep the records," she'd say of my holdings. "You have to do them now. It's too much for me."

Why hadn't I heard what she was really saying? *Let me show you how to do this, now while I'm still able. Let me teach you now, before I die.*

Perhaps she sensed that she was going, or maybe she was covering all her bases, "in case." Whatever the reason, we had been given a warning, followed by the miracle of extra time—of extra good time, not sick time. We had been given the chance to say goodbye. We had told each other we loved each other. She had seen all her loved ones, held them.

But as she grew progressively weaker, it became clear to me that the end was near. And as she anxiously climbed in and out of bed, every two or three minutes, for hours, I knew what I had to do. I knew what would work, what would calm her down and comfort her. I also knew that Grandma loved life and thanked God for each day. But now she was suffering, not living.

As I sat alone next to my grandmother's bed, she slowly opened her eyes and looked at me imploringly.

Summoning all of her energy, she spoke for the first and only time that day. "Patti, I'm so sick."

I took her hand and looked into her eyes. Yes, I knew what to do for her. What I had to do. What she had once done for me.

I was about eight years old at the time, maybe a little younger, and was sure I was going to die. I had a stomach flu, the kind where you retch and retch until you feel you'll pass out. My stomach was rolling and churning; I was dizzy, too dizzy to move; and I was shaking with fever. It was in a country house we had rented, about forty-five minutes from the city. I wanted my mother. She had been commuting back and forth to Manhattan, for me, to support us. But you can't reason with a sick child. I wanted my mother; that was all.

My grandmother called her at her office, and my mother said she'd be on the next train out. But time moved more slowly than I had ever known it to. I wanted to sleep more than anything, other than to feel better and to see my mother. But I couldn't get comfortable, much less sleep, with the waves of nausea engulfing me. I moaned and twisted, waiting for my mother to arrive.

It was then that my grandmother climbed into bed with me. *Fearless*, I remember thinking. After all, she could catch this thing. But she lay down next to me and held me, anyway. Only then was I able to finally drift off. Slowly, very slowly, I felt sleep replace the nausea. And, safe in my grandmother's arms, the sick restlessness became a restful sleep, and I began to feel better.

Sitting next to my grandmother's bed, I leaned down and gently kissed her forehead.

Then I climbed into bed with her. She moved over willingly. I held her in my arms as she had done for me that day so long ago. I closed my eyes tightly, trying hard not to cry. The tears came, anyway, but fell silently. Grandma moved into a snuggle position with me, resting her head against my chest, finally comfortable. She squeezed my hand and smiled. Smiled! As we held onto each other, she grew quiet and still. Within minutes, she was asleep.

—*Pat Gallant*

Postscript: My beloved grandmother, Beth Beyer Selverne, passed away quietly in her sleep the next day.

Calling Out for Angels

Not all angels wanted humans to be created, legend tells us. Some felt that humans would be liars, others that humans would be too quarrelsome. Legend also has it that God was unhappy with the doubting angels and consumed them by the fire of his little finger. But one angel, named Labbiel, supported the creation of humans. He was rewarded, anointed the keeper of all medical remedies used on Earth, and his name was changed to Raphael, the rescuer and healer. Raphael's band of angels agreed to watch over humans and to reveal their secrets to them.

I'm thinking of this legend as Ann and I sit on her balcony on a June evening, the one evening it hasn't stormed all spring. We have reshuffled the small balcony to make room for her wheelchair so she can watch the sunset. With her sunglasses on, she holds her face up to the sun streaking the sky purple and orange over the National Cathedral in Washington, D.C. I move my chair to face her and feel the warmth on my back.

"It feels good," she says, smiling, gazing from behind dark glasses out into the air high above the city. She sighs, "This balcony gives me so much pleasure."

Finally, she has let me bring dinner and have a "girls' night out" on the balcony. She has been in a dark mood for weeks while considering yet another surgery, another part of a body going wrong after a spinal stroke. She has decided against the surgery, even though she probably needs it. Perhaps the decision has called for a celebration of sorts and she has let me join her. She sits with her Rob Roy, I with my glass of wine.

They say the angel Raphael sits behind those who are ill and in need. I keep hoping. Every day I wish for change, a breakthrough. Still, Ann sits in a wheelchair, this energetic friend whose high heels I can still hear clicking down the hallway in the high school we taught in. This smart woman who left teaching to others, entered the business world, and with her great entrepreneurial spirit, had great success. Thank God she did. Who prepares for a spinal stroke, ever, let alone in your fifties?

She is talking about old times. The school where we met. The "older" male teacher with the buzz cut who made us miserable until we filled his beakers with strange concoctions. The principal with white socks and a terror of teenagers. We are laughing as hard thirty years later as we had laughed then. I am also keeping an eye out for Raphael or at least an angel or two from his band of lesser types who guard over humans.

I watch this brave friend who has reworked her life with dignity each time pieces of her body succumb to a different illness. I see how tired she is as she firmly grasps the arms of the wheelchair with each hand and hoists herself up off the seat, locking her arms.

"I have to stretch sometimes," she says. "Don't mind me."

"Can I help?" I ask. No, she shakes her head vehemently, dangles a moment, then lowers herself back onto the wheelchair seat.

The conversation ebbs and flows. We talk about the investments we share with the same broker. I am cursing; she is laughing.

"Things have to get better," she says about the market. "It's all in the stars," she says, admonishing me not to get so frustrated.

I watch my former science-teacher-turned-mystical friend chuckling in the sunset.

"It's chilly," I say. The sky is now only blues and purples. "Let's stay until the last bit of purple is gone," she says. "You know I love purple. I don't want to miss a moment of it."

"Your outfit matches the sky," I say.

Her closet has been cleansed of anything but loose purple clothes—easy to get into and out of.

We sit a moment longer. Finally, she okays the move back inside. We maneuver on the small balcony until she can push herself into the apartment.

"What a heavenly night," she says, glancing back at the scattering of clouds still glistening above the cathedral.

I stand a moment longer, looking out over the dusky sky.

"What are you doing standing there?" she asks. "You were the one who wanted to come in."

"Raphael, where is the healing? Where are the remedies?" I whisper into the sky, my back turned so that my tough, tired friend can't hear. "Come soon . . . you've just got to. If you're too busy, just please send one of your lesser guys. Anything at all to help."

I take one more look for signs in the sky, then turn and follow the wheelchair into the apartment.

Over the proceeding year, things go from bad to worse. On a dark January morning, when Ann's caretaker calls me from the hospital, I really start calling out for help from above.

"She's in a coma. I couldn't wake her this morning," the caretaker whispers from the waiting room. "They say she won't last the day out."

"I'll be right over," I say.

Before jumping into my car, I put a couple of poems in my purse to read, just in case. I sit with Ann in the critical care unit off and on for three days. Although she has left every kind of directive, once you are in the hospital, they have to try to keep you alive. She is hooked up to many machines in the little cubicle.

I try talking to her—no response. I call out to angels again—no response. Finally, I ask the nurse if I can read to her.

"Sure," she says, "it can't hurt. You won't disturb anyone."

I lean over and whisper into Ann's ear, "Hi, it's me. I've come to read to you." I repeat it as near to her ear as I can, maneuvering around the machines.

Suddenly, she murmurs . . . well, not murmurs exactly, but there are sounds, some movement.

I start to read, first a poem I wrote about us both catching up at a doctor's appointment, then another one I wrote to cheer her up when she first got sick, about purple, her favorite color. As I read "More things should be purple," there is more movement.

"She recognizes you . . . or at least she is making some attempt to come out of the vegetative state," says the nurse. She commands me to keep reading.

And I do, every day for an hour or so. I come to the hospital, sit at her bedside, and read. I read when she is moved from critical care to a regular room. I read when she is sent to hospice. I read when hospice decides she is too well to stay in hospice and she is moved to a nursing home, which she despises, but where she lives for the next year. Ann swears that my reading to her brought her back.

I laugh. "Maybe it was angels," I say, since she knew that I was writing about angels. "Shall I read you the angel story I am writing about you?" I ask her.

"No, now I only want you to read to me in the hospital. Read to me only when I need to be brought back," she says. "Let's just talk."

And we do, for hours—about our lives, our decisions, what has gone right and what has gone wrong. And we talk about her pain and the spasms she endures from her paralyzed legs.

We talk, and I do not read to her, until the day Ann calls in a hoarse voice after trying for days to get the nursing home to run tests on her. She knew she was developing an infection. The nursing home did nothing for days, but now, she tells me, they are finally taking her to the hospital. They waited too long. By the time she arrives at the hospital, she is in critical condition with sepsis throughout her body.

I go to the hospital armed with my poems and stories about her. I wipe her face, hold her swollen hand. But this time, when I lean near and ask if she wants me to read to her, she becomes agitated, even in her deep coma. Although her arms are restrained to hold the needles bringing her fluids and antibiotics, she yanks at the restraints.

I sit beside her bed quietly. I do not read. I think about our forty years of friendship and how much I will miss her, but she has suffered enough, more than anyone should have to endure. I grow certain that she is telling me to let her go, to leave her in peace. I sit thinking about Raphael and what he would do. I wonder where he and his angels are now. After sitting beside her for an hour or so, I decide to head home. As I tip-toe out of the room, I glance back. She seems calmer, almost smiling. And I swear I hear her say, "Do not bring me back. There are angels where I am headed."

—*Davi Walders*

Some names in this story have been changed to protect the privacy of those individuals and their loved ones.

A Fitting Farewell

The minister stood behind the podium above the open casket and called the names of Chester's immediate family.

My mind flew back to when we were kids. Chester was Mama's brother, but he was nearer my age. I visited my grandmother's house often because I had no one to play with at home. I laid my dolls aside, took up my cap pistol, donned my cowboy hat, and loaded my BB gun. Chester and I were best buddies. My name should have been in that sister list.

The minister said, "Chester has left us many fond memories."

A childhood memory came rushing back. I was a little girl, about four, spending the night at my grandmother's house. I awoke one morning with Chester bending over me and shaking me, his dark, wavy, uncombed hair and pale blue eyes showing signs he'd recently awakened.

"I want you to cry with a belly-ache and say you need me to stay home from school today," he whispered.

"Huh?" I sat up in bed, rubbing my eyes, thinking he'd gone crazy or something. "What're ya talking about?"

"Mother is working in the tobacco patch with Daddy today. I heard her say it. So, if you cry real hard, I can stay here and take care of you. Then we can play all day long."

"But that would be a lie," I replied and turned over in bed, snuggling back into my pillow.

He shook me awake again. "Do you want to stay home and play, or do you want to go to the hot old field?"

I peeked at him through squinted eyes. "When we play cowboys, you always make me be the bad guy. I gotta be the good guy this time or I won't do it."

Chester promised I could be the good cowboy.

I knew I shouldn't do it—lying was bad—but it sounded better than sitting under a tree while Mother (as we all, even I, called my grandmother) sowed or planted or whatever she had to do. Besides, I had my new Red Ryder BB gun and a cowboy hat; I'd make a good cowboy in that get-up. I thought about it a long time, and sure enough, my stomach did begin to hurt. The more I thought about it, the more it hurt, and I began to cry.

Mother allowed Chester to stay home from school.

"I'm a bad cowboy. I'll take that gun. Give me the hat, too," he growled as he tied me to a tree.

Of course, I couldn't tattle on him, because I was supposed to be in bed sick.

Randal, the minister, who was Chester's nephew, said, "Chester was a clever man. He could outwit and outfox anyone."

I smiled at that. I could remember only one time when I outwitted him.

"Oh, come on, Chester, let's play doctor. I don't wanta play cowboys and Indians. Look, I got some pills to give you." I held out a handful of hard candy.

"Well, okay. But you give me all the pills at once, so I'll get well real soon."

I knew he was going to get all my candy and run off. But I fixed him. I had a handful of sheep balls in my other hand. He opened his mouth right up, ready and eager for his medicine. Then I switched the candy balls for the sheep balls, plopping the little round, black sheep droppings into his mouth instead. He was really mad. So mad I thought he was going to hit me, but he didn't.

"Chester could fix anything that was broken . . . or he could find a way of bypassing the problem."

I almost giggled out loud when Randal said that.

One cold winter night when Chester was twelve or thirteen, his dad, my grandpa, having had a few too many swigs of whiskey, became too inebriated to drive us home. Chester volunteered for the job. Chester's sister Sarah, Mother, and I huddled in the back seat under the cover of a wool lap rug.

Chester had a heavy foot even then. He swerved the old dilapidated Model-A around one curve after another in the gravel road. Finally Mother couldn't stand it any longer. "Son, you must slow down. You're scaring the kids half to death."

"But, Mother," Chester answered. "I have to drive fast. We're almost out of gas, and I want to hurry home before we run out."

My naïve grandmother contemplated for a minute. "Well, son, in that case—Lord, I never thought I'd ever tell a child to drive fast—but, if that's the case, then you'd better hurry it up and get us home." She'd believed every word he said.

Randal went on. "Chester was always ready to lend a helping hand to anybody in need."

Once he loaned me his hand, literally, when I really needed it. We were taking a shortcut through a neighbor's field. A humongous, white-faced, red bull with huge horns stomped and snorted and made a lunge for us. Chester grabbed my hand and jumped onto an old hay baler, pulling me up with him. We sat in the hot sun for what seemed like hours. The bull stomped and butted the machine, but finally gave up and wandered away.

"Quick!" Chester said. "Run!"

We made a mad dash for the fence. We heard the bull bellowing and running behind us. I ran as fast as my short, chubby legs would move, but the bull kept getting closer. Chester was older, leaner, and faster, but he didn't leave me. He dragged me with him across the field, yelling "Hold on to me!" the whole way. Then he hefted me over the top line of barbed wire as he hurtled over it himself just as the bull rammed into the fence. Randal concluded with, "Chester lived a fulfilled life."

While Chester's life had been filled with fast cars, rowdy friends, and traipsing on the wild side, I had matured into a more reserved adult. Still, we remained best friends. It took six children, three marriages, and a bad heart for Chester to redirect his thrill-seeking nature on hunting and fishing rather than on his previous fascinations.

Randal discreetly omitted that part of his uncle's life. Instead, he mentioned how much his children would miss him.

Chester loved his children with a passion. Yet, he expected his firstborn son to inherit at least a small amount of his grit. He didn't expect Donnie to partake in all his rascally ways, but he was a little disappointed that Donnie had inherited his mother's calmer, quieter mannerisms.

By the time the funeral service ended, the nostalgic reminiscence it evoked had given me the opportunity to relish the close relationship that Chester and I had shared.

Chester died in 1999, at age sixty-three, from a heart attack. His death, like his life, was fast-paced; his burial was even more so.

"Where in the world is that hearse driver taking us?" my daughter exclaimed. "I think he's lost.

We were part of a long procession of mourners in numerous cars, driving in and out of traffic and on and off expressway ramps, with other vehicles constantly breaking into our caravan. Many of our rural family members were unfamiliar with driving in the city. I'd lived in the area for years, and even I was getting panicky trying to keep up with the funeral procession.

Then, to make matters worse, a young man in a fast car decided that he, too, would break into our line-up. He nearly clipped the front bumper of my car as he whipped in and out of the procession. Then he attempted to whip in front of Donald, but Donald speeded up, blocking the intruder's way into our lane. At that point, the confused hearse driver came to a stop, for some unknown reason, leaving some of us on the exit ramp and still others stopped on the expressway. The man in the speeding car stopped too. He jumped out of his automobile and ran up to Donald's car. When Donald rolled down the window to see what he wanted, the man punched Donald in the face. Chester came alive again! The usually mild-mannered Donald sprang from the car with flying fists. After we finally got Donald off the guy and back into the car, the young man muttered, "I didn't know it was a funeral procession. I thought those blue flags were Kentucky Wildcat pennants." I supposed he was not a U of K fan.

By then, the whole family was hysterical. The last thing we'd expected on that somber day was for the entire funeral procession to be stopped on an expressway while two men rolled in the grass, fists flailing. Least of all now—with Chester dead. But no one fainted or passed out. And we finally made it to the cemetery.

Once we'd all gathered around the gravesite, the minister proceeded to say a few words over the closed casket. He looked down very solemnly and then up again, and closed the service with a slight smile on his lips. "All I have to add is, Uncle Chester sure went out with a bang."

Donnie's mom, tears flowing down her face, put her arms around Donnie's neck and said, "Son, your daddy would be proud today."

Someone began a contagious chuckle that passed through the group of mourners. We stood there for several minutes, laughing out loud as the tears streamed from our eyes. It was a fitting farewell to Chester—my uncle, my brother, my friend.

—*Jean Kinsey*

My Ever Muse

As a poet, I frame the story of my husband's illness and death with an excerpt from Walt Whitman:

I have perceiv'd that to be with those I like is enough.

To stop in company with the rest at evening is enough,

To be surrounded by beautiful, curious, breathing, laughing flesh is enough,

To pass among them, or touch any one, or rest my arm ever so lightly round his or her neck for a moment—what is this, then?

I do not ask any more delight—I swim in it, as in a sea.

Richie, my husband of forty years, savored life and swam in it, always magnifying joys and facing problems with grit. He was long on delight and short on complaints and blame. Richie did not hold grudges and had no guile. The transparency of his face told you what he was thinking and feeling. Richie was well known for his acts of great decency and charity. Years ago, I wrote a piece called "Gentle Jim and the Christmas Coat," which tells the story of Richie taking the coat off his back and placing it on a shivering, apparently mentally ill man, roaming the streets of Portsmouth, New Hampshire. No one who knew my Richie was surprised to hear about it. He was not a saint but speckled with imperfections as we all are. Of course, our marriage was not perfect, either. After all, it was a marriage, with all that implies, but arguments were short-lived and never malicious.

Richie died of lung cancer in August of 2008. He never smoked, and doctors did not find employment risks. His father had died of prostate cancer, and Richie was vigilant about yearly preventive blood work for that. Yet, out of nowhere, we received the jolt of a lung cancer diagnosis. It was a kick in the teeth. We were joyfully planning a travel itinerary for his recent retirement. As a freelance writer and poet, I have formed friendships across the country at conferences and readings, and now my literary companions would get to know my sweet Richie . . . we thought.

It started with a dry cough in October, when he was diagnosed with the flu. By November, with the coughing increasing, an X-ray was taken and he was told he had pneumonia. After two trials of antibiotics, he continued to cough and to lose weight, so a biopsy was ordered. But it was too late; the cancer had spread to the lymph nodes in his neck. An MRI revealed a tumor the size of a soft ball surrounded by smaller tumors. In early December, a grim-faced surgeon explained to Richie that he suffered from stage four, metastasized, nonsmoker's lung cancer. The surgeon was barely audible when he uttered the torturous death sentence, and we all waited uncomfortably for the moment to pass.

Finally, the surgeon said, "You must be angry, and very frightened."

Richie reflected for a moment and said, "No."

A long, awkward silence passed. The surgeon and I looked at the floor.

Then Richie said, "I'm happy God gave me a life to lose in the first place."

I knew then that my sweetheart would die in a unique, courageous, and gracious way—just as he had lived. No fear. No blame. No cursing. No self-pity. Instead, Richie uttered thanksgiving and praises for his Maker and an unabashed gratitude for the opportunity of tasting human life.

Richie reinforced that this would be his approach to dying on the drive home.

"Hey, honey, I'm sixty-six. It's not like I'm twenty-six or six," he said. "I've had a good life. And I'm not leaving young children. That counts for a lot. We've had forty good years together. I don't have any complaints."

From that point forward, Richie focused on life, on our life together, not on death, and I felt a relief and comfort for him, for us, in that. I relied on an intuition that told me he would die with the least suffering possible for himself and for the rest of us. Regrets and sorrow surfaced, of course, as the realization of how seriously ill he was set in and the changes of lifestyle became real. We cancelled our trip to China just in time to receive a full refund on the deposit. A road trip across the United States and Canada to meet my literary friends dissolved, and a volunteer stint with the Benedictine Sisters in Mount Angel, Oregon, would never be. Friends cried on the phone with us as our plans to camp at Yosemite together that summer faded.

I felt sad and angry as I watched what I perceived to be carefree couples in stores, at church, at the beach, and at movies. Their happiness made me jealous. But unhappy couples angered me, too. I fought impulses to shout at those I heard arguing, "Do you know how precious life is? You're wasting time! Don't be stupid!"

I felt bitter and cheated, knowing that for the next year or two we would be immersed in a draining, ugly battle for survival, spending the short remainder of Richie's life between our cottage and the hospital and specialists' offices. *What if he didn't make it?* I'd worry. Then I'd pick myself up and visualize him "making it." I was measuring life in length rather than quality. But Richie would soon teach me the wonder of his beautiful life.

In July, he was too weak to travel, so friends from California came to meet him. We all spoke openly, and at a cookout he told them, "I'm ready to die, to move on. I don't want to cling."

The next morning, over oatmeal and a poached egg, he informed me, "You're fired. I need round-the-clock nursing and daily visits from a doc and complicated medicines. And I need to free you for living."

"Home hospice can be all over this cottage at all hours," I argued. They'd been coming to the house a few times a week; they could come more, as much as he needed. "Don't leave," I pleaded.

I couldn't budge him.

Later that morning, he asked Dr. Jones to place him in hospice.

"Priscilla's a poet, not a nurse," he told him. "Our cottage is our sweet home, and I do not want a wheelchair or commode or oxygen or any medical stuff happening in our home. Please, place me in Hyder Family Hospice Center . . . today."

Then my mild-mannered, sweet-tempered Richie shocked the doctor and his nurses by raising his voice and proclaiming, "Today, Doc, today. Please make the arrangements."

That evening at the hospice center, Richie shifted his bony rear-end around in the bed until he felt comfortable. He appraised the layout of the room, especially the proximity of the toilet. He looked at birdhouses in the yard.

Then he said to himself more than to me, "Yeah, this will do," and let out the deepest, longest sigh I've ever heard.

He was settling in to die, and we both knew it.

That week, Richie began detaching and asked me to remove photos, flowers, cards, and other such from his room.

"Take them home, hon, and make the cottage pretty. They remind me too much of this life, and I'm planning my trip to somewhere else. Tell everyone thank you and not to send any more."

Richie did not have the year or two we'd hoped for in the beginning. Eight months after his diagnosis, he died at Hyder House. He was out of my care for only eleven days, and he'd finely tuned and designed those days with utmost consideration for me, our son and daughter, his family, and our friends. As usual, he placed himself last.

When hospice staff overheard Richie inquire as to our cat, Ceesco, and say how much he missed him, they encouraged me to bring Ceesco Cat to visit him. I started setting it up, and he was happy. But then he stopped me.

"Don't do it. He gets all nervous in the carrier, and his tongue sticks out. It's awful. Please, don't upset the cat."

Richie didn't simply talk of loving his pet—he *showed* his love for Ceesco and spared him discomfort. He put the cat ahead of himself.

Love was seldom a noun for Richie; it was a verb he practiced daily. Can you imagine the lengths he went to in order to spare all of us unnecessary suffering? As my husband diminished our marital bond, he intensified his bond with hospice staff. Richie took all of us—wife, children, mother, sister, friends—off the hook. No demands for round-the-clock bedside vigils, or daily visitors, or last-minute rushes to his death bed, or requests to die at home. No one who loved him had anything to prove.

My beloved stepped forward boldly and peacefully, considering others.

When asked by his chaplain, physician, and social worker to confirm his readiness for dying, he told them, "I was ready a month ago."

That evening, he asked me not to visit the next day because it would be another humid, beach day. It seemed outrageous and nonsensical to me.

"Please, honey, go swimming. Have friends for a cookout. Walk the woods with Ceesco."

While he lay dying? I should live while he dies?

When I protested, he responded, "Why should two be indoors on a beautiful day? Will you please live in the world out there and do what I can't? Isn't it enough that one of us is dying? Will you live, please, and I don't mean just exist. Please, enjoy life."

It was a tall order, which, at first, seemed counterintuitive. Upon reflection, I realized that, although it was a countercultural response, it made perfect intuitive sense. Richie needed my permission to die unhindered, and I needed his permission to live in the same liberated way. So we shook off conflicts of attachment and pressures of societal expectations and began our separate journeys. Richie surrendered his mere carcass to hospice care, and I supported him in that. He nudged me toward a future here, and I stepped along living, just as he moved along dying—without each other's physical accompaniment.

Our life together had been unusual. Why shouldn't our separation by death be equally as eccentric? It is who we are, who we were. Richie was not a saint, as I said earlier, though it is tempting to sanctify him, to hold on to him and build a shrine, but that is not the truth of him and of us. My husband was my personal hero, my Amazing Guy. We made necessary changes to better enjoy living together and grew up and became each other's second spouses in a way. Why mention it? I believe none of you can savor the sweetness of our relationship if I do not acknowledge the bitter. Richie and I enjoyed strong spiritual identities during our forty years and worked not to blame each other for human failings, instead assuming individual responsibility for our personal growth.

I miss Richie's physical presence, but I know we consist of body, psyche, and spirit, and I sense a presence of his spirit flitting about me daily, poking in as a muse to my work. Richie's spirit was alongside me as I wrote these lines:

"Tenor of Care"

Devotion tumbles tenderly

into the ears

while obligation . . . deafens.

Richie and I are occupied: he in building a new life and I immersed in completing this one. For now, we meet in altered states until we catch up to each other. I love that he was able to consider himself and his *self*, ultimately. Yes, it was time for us to choose separate paths—soul mates psychically and physically separated but still connected spiritually. I don't know what responsibilities or joys are coming Richie's way today, but I have a deadline to meet for a prose piece and friends to enjoy at the theater tonight. Off I go!

—Priscilla Carr

So Far and Yet So Near

It is Easter Sunday, 1965. I am five and you are seven. We wear identical outfits: pale yellow puffy dresses with embroidered daisies at the neckline, floppy white hats, white gloves, and shiny white patent leather shoes. We could be twins. Of course, this is only an illusion. I am destined to be a tomboy with ripped, stained clothes, while you are destined to be a princess with angel wings. But for today, Easter Sunday 1965, we are exactly the same. You smile down at me, your front two teeth missing. I smile back, wishing my front teeth were missing too.

You're in third grade, I'm in first. After school, we sit on the ground playing with Barbie and Ken, sharing a giant bag of M&Ms. I don't mind being Ken all the time. When you play the teacher, I am your student. I sit cross-legged on the bed, studying the way you hold the ruler, tapping it lightly on the blackboard. My eyes are glued to "10 × 6 = 60," as if it were a million dollars. You are my hero.

When we are ten and twelve, you won't play Barbie and Ken with me anymore. You are always in a bad mood, and I don't understand what is wrong with you. You make a ton of friends with little effort, while I struggle to make even one friend.

As I sit across from you in the tiny bedroom we share, wearing my Joe Namath T-shirt, I pretend to be shuffling my baseball cards. I watch as you sort through your flowered dresses and all those shoes that you are beginning to collect. Your teeth are so big and white, and when you are on the phone with one of your many friends, your laugh is so hearty and loud. When I have my privacy, I try to copy you in every way.

Even though your social calendar is full, you still make some time for me. Together, we watch *The Brady Bunch* and *The Partridge Family*, once again sharing a giant bag of M&Ms. You warn me that you have dibs on David. Afterward, you patiently show me how to straighten my hair by rolling it around orange-juice cans. You show me how to coat my face with Noxema Skin Cream to ward off bad skin. I slowly drift off to sleep, breathing in the intoxicating scent and wishing I were you.

One day, you allow me to tag along with you and your friends to a David Cassidy concert. When

David throws a sweat-stained paper towel into the audience, you are able to score part of it from one of your friends who had better seats than we did. You don't hesitate to give me a piece. It's the size of a postage stamp, but it means the world to me.

When I am fifteen and you are seventeen, it becomes unbearable to share a bedroom with you anymore. We are opposites in every way possible. I hate your Elton John and Bee Gees, and you hate my Led Zeppelin and Kiss. I hate your chinos and Mary Jane's, and you hate my tight Jordache, my impossibly straight hair, and my flawless skin. I still have no friends, and you still have too many to count. You come home at night, plop yourself down on the bed, and sigh too loudly with exhaustion from your busy day. This angers me and causes me to constantly roll my eyes at you, as if I will have you forever.

As we go through our twenties and thirties, we see the world with such different eyes. We don't agree on anything. On our politics, our lifestyles, and everything in between, we are polar opposites. We have little time for one another; our jobs and separate lives keep us at a respectful distance. We still silently roll our eyes at one another through the phone lines, still assuming we will have each other forever. During this time, I often wonder if things will ever be the way they once were between us, so long ago.

When we are in our forties, we sit side by side at chemotherapy, our arms touching slightly, with nowhere to go. Your social calendar has come to a sudden halt, and we are forced to have time for one another again. You don't know it, but I am once again studying you. I think I am trying to remember the details so I won't forget you, when the time comes.

Everything about you is so beautiful, each detail magnificent—your teeth so white, your eyes so blue. Your wig is slightly lop-sided and you are wearing a bright red sweater as you write out your Christmas cards with your free hand. Every now and then you raise your head to laugh at something Joy Behar says on the television. Oh, my God, your laugh! How is it possible that I can suddenly love everything about you once again?

We sit and talk and *agree* about everything under the sun now. We laugh and make jokes while we share a bag of M&Ms, our hands grazing as they bump into one another. We say we love each other all the time.

What I don't tell you is that I have had a secret dream since forever. In my mind, I had it all planned out. One day, when we were finished living our separate lives, we'd once more have all the time in the world for one another and we would agree on everything.

As I sit next to you at chemotherapy, I have never felt closer to you. It is as though we are exactly the same, like all those years ago on Easter Sunday 1965.

I will not get to tell you this, but the days we spend at chemotherapy are the best days of my life.

I am forty-eight years old, and I miss you so much. But here's why I feel so blessed: I know now that, if you had lived to be 100, we never would have gotten to that place I used to dream of, the place where we were when we sat side by side at your chemotherapy sessions.

I suppose, in the grand scheme of things, our relationship was never defined by our differences. Relationships aren't perfect, after all. I used to have so many regrets about our relationship, and now I have none. I will always be grateful for the chance to bond with you when you were sick.

Sometimes when I think about you now, the lights flicker. I think it might be you. Is it you? I hope so. Even though you are gone, I always feel close to you, my big sister with the hearty laugh. My hero.

—*Carolyn McGovern*

The Dark Green

"Hon, what should I wear today?" Michael asked, sticking his head into the bathroom which was still steamy from our showers.

"A suit, baby. What else?" I answered, not looking away from the spot I had wiped clear on the mirror. I was applying concealer to the puffy, dark circles that had made themselves at home under my eyes during the past four days.

"Which one?" came his voice, unrelenting.

"You could've given this some thought last night." I was tired of holding up, tired of holding on.

"Well, I can't wear the same one I wore to the wake . . . " his voice trailed off. "People would be sure to notice, don't you think?"

I put down the concealer and picked up the slim tube of black mascara, wondering if it was waterproof.

My husband's wardrobe concerns were not high on my priority list at the moment.

"What are you gonna wear?" he asked when I didn't answer. By now he had moved his entire body into the room, no longer just his head.

"The dark green suit."

The last time I had worn that suit was still a vivid memory, and I floated back into it now. I had attended the funeral service for my friend John's father. After many years of slow deterioration, Rosario had finally succumbed to kidney disease. Once a strapping man, a retired construction worker, Rosario seemed to shrink along with his kidney function, and his illness had touched a chord with me. A gentle man, he had always had a smile and some pleasant conversation to share. Like most Italian men of his generation, he didn't strike me as overly expressive, but the quiet warmth he exuded made me sure that those who counted him as a friend considered themselves blessed. The fact that there was a crowd of people at his service served to confirm my assessment. John's wife delivered a loving eulogy for her father-in-law, and empathy welled in me for the grieving family, whose faces clearly revealed the pain of their loss. At the conclusion of the service, as we mourners quietly trailed the family out of the church, Tina, a mutual acquaintance, intercepted me just steps from my car.

"I'm so sorry to hear that your father isn't well," she said.

"Oh, he'll be alright," I answered reflexively, recoiling from her tone and her words, which were too serious, too scary. I jingled my keys, impatient to escape this conversation. "He's going to be fine. I'll tell him you asked for him, though," I said, backing away from her.

Once I was safe in my car, I quickly popped the transmission into gear. Feeling the tires slip against the pavement, I peeled out of the parking lot with a degree of speed that was inappropriate for the occasion, my mind focused on denying the comparison Tina had implied. As I followed the creeping line of cars to the cemetery, my thoughts ran to the obvious differences between Dad's situation and Rosario's illness. My dad was going to get a liver transplant, like his brother had successfully done years before, and then he'd be back to normal. His hepatitis had been under control for so long that he wasn't going to succumb now. Dad was a survivor, and this period of feeling less than perfect was just a bump in the road.

When we arrived at the cemetery, funeral parlor staff directed each automobile to a parking spot. Getting out of my car carefully, I made a point to avoid Tina and anyone else who might speak to me about my dad by hanging back on the fringes of the group. After the priest delivered the final blessing and concluded the graveside service with a booming "Amen," I waited even longer for most of the crowd to disperse before going forward to offer my condolences to the family.

My heart wrenched as I approached Rosario's widow, her devastation clear in the quivering of her lips. Whereas my words of sympathy to Maria were soft whispers, my handclasp was tight, the physical contact firmly declaring what my voice, choked with emotion, could not. When I hugged John, my eyes filled with tears that matched his, and then I stumbled away from them, my heels catching in the soft earth.

My thoughts had returned to my dad as soon as I navigated out of the maze of the cemetery. Instead of heading directly home to change out of my high heels, hose, and the dark green suit, I turned off at the exit for my parent's house so I could check in on Dad. He was lying down on the sagging corduroy couch with my mom's multicolored afghan pulled up to his chest, even though the room was toasty, but he sat up and attempted a smile when I knocked at the unlocked slider and walked in.

"How're you feeling today, Dad?"

"I feel okay," he said, but the whites of his eyes couldn't truthfully be described by that color anymore and the thinness of his face contradicted my memory of the vibrant man he'd been only two years ago.

I made us both a cup of chamomile tea and sat beside him, cradling the warm ceramic mug in my hands.

"You look sharp," he said, shifting the focus away from himself, in true Dad fashion. "I like that shade of green on you. Much better than black."

Delighted with the gift of his pleasure, I chose to overlook the fact that the suit was a little outdated, its skirt a tad too long and its lapels a tad too wide.

"Not black?" Michael asked, his puzzled voice bringing me back to the present.

"No. Dad hated black," I said, my voice trembling.

Then, remembering that my dad always stood by his convictions—one of his many admirable qualities that I meant to speak about in his eulogy that day—and knowing that he would want me to stand by mine, my voice grew strong. "The dark green is just right."

—*Nancy Antonietti*

Alone in a Crowd

A man in the back of the room is wearing flip-flops. He's sitting cross-legged, letting one of the flip-flops dangle off his big toe, revealing a plaid, cloth-lined sole. His suit makes the flip-flops seem even more inappropriate for a funeral. For as comfortable as he appears with his footwear choice, he shifts around and looks as if the suit may be made of sandpaper instead of gabardine. He dabs constantly at his nose and swollen eyes.

A seventeen-year-old girl sitting toward the middle of the room is shushing a chubby infant. A sometimes friend of my brother, she stopped coming around as her belly swelled because the neighbors were whispering their suspicions about paternity just loudly enough for her to hear. That my brother was a good kid, just a friend to a girl in trouble, wasn't enough to quell the rumors. He'd been able to ignore them, always appearing to slough off others' opinions like dead skin. She took on the embarrassment for him until it was too much to bear, and soon we stopped seeing her at our dinner table.

Near the back third of the room sits a boy of twenty, my brother's age. He'd probably chosen to sit there because, for as long as I'd known him, he'd always been polite and he'd likely realized that his mohawk would prevent someone behind him from seeing the service. Still, he hadn't chosen the last row, something not lost on me. Someone who'd melted plastic army men in the sun with my brother when they were six could never sit with his back to the wall today. He'd need to be closer, near enough to see my brother's face. His big sister, the one who'd moved all the way to California, had flown in on the red-eye the minute she'd heard, just to make it to the service.

My brother's boss sits near the front. She's a Chinese woman, exquisitely dressed in a suit from her own label, a company she'd founded as an immigrant five years ago when she'd hired my brother as a stock boy, an afterschool job. He prided himself on his wardrobe from work—although, you'd never know if he, now as her most trusted manager, would show up there on any given Tuesday in cashmere or in baggy jeans and a crumpled T-shirt.

I'm sitting in the back row. I've moved my seat twice. I was sitting up front, but I had to move. They never do the makeup right on people; I stayed up all night last night worrying about his. I was right to worry. He looks weird, and it's not how I want to remember my brother. So I moved to the back where I could get a blurrier, more distorted picture. He's wearing a turtleneck to cover the bruises, which makes everything seem worse; I can't remember seeing him wear a turtleneck in his whole life. The entire thing is surreal, and no matter what I do, I'm afraid that, now that I've seen him this way, I won't remember him the other way, the way I knew him two weeks ago.

As I look around, it occurs to me that no two people here have anything in common other than my brother. The Air Force officer, sitting stock straight in service dress in the front row would pass the mohawk boy on the street without a cursory glance. Mr. Flip-Flop and the girl with black onyx-colored hair and a nose stud might meet in a bar and go home together, but she'd regret him in the morning, wondering what attracted her to someone so preppy.

I hadn't been able to make sense of much since my phone rang a week ago and I'd heard what my brother had done. Now that I see this room, with every seat filled, I'm even more confused.

The room pulses with the shared heartbeats of the mourners. Each heart there is broken just a little bit for what happened just a few days earlier. The only other funeral I've ever been to was for my grandfather, and while I remember it being quiet, too, it was a serene quiet. The quiet in this room is a shared stunned silence and a common understanding that none of us understands one another or what has happened. Looking around the room, with no two people seeming to have anything in common, it occurs to me that we have the deepest of commonalities to share, yet we sit silent in our grief, dabbing at our eyes and stifling our sobs so as not to disturb one another. My brother loved everyone in this room, and they loved him, and we are all grieving the same grief.

"David was alone in this world," the preacher begins. "How else could he have done this to himself?"

I get up and leave, waiting outside for the service to end. There are many lies we hear when someone we love takes his own life, most of them from ourselves. I can't handle another.

When the rest of the mourners leave, I return to speak to my brother. "I'm sorry you felt alone. It was the one thing you never were."

With the first truth told, the tears fall. Now, I can begin to say goodbye and finally start to heal.

—Rachel McClain

Hospice for the Holidays

My mom called at four thirty on the afternoon of December twenty-first. "Your dad's home from the hospital; he's on hospice."

Dad had been diagnosed with esophageal cancer months earlier, and now he had been sent home to die.

That night, I caught the red-eye flight from Los Angeles to Cleveland, arriving three days before Christmas. Though I tried to make it home once a year, I had not shared a Christmas with my family in more than a decade. The thought of crowded airports, cramped coach cabins, and the bitter cold of Ohio in December had trumped any desire to spend the holidays east of the Mississippi. Now, arriving at my girlhood home at seven in the morning, I shivered in the sub-zero temperature. The pine trees lining the driveway were draped in heavy snow, and my boots crunched on the rock salt covering the sidewalk.

Warmth and a wave of nostalgia greeted me when I stepped through the front door. My mom was in the midst of picking up a screaming teapot. The sink was half filled with dishes, and an unread newspaper lay on the kitchen table. Both of my sisters sat at the kitchen table, sipping heavily creamed coffee. The status quo was interrupted by my arrival into the kitchen. We group-hugged, laughed, and avoided the obvious.

After I answered the usual polite questions about my flight, airline food, and the enviable California weather, the conversation lagged.

Finally, my mom whispered, "Your dad's downstairs." This was Mom's way of saying, "Go downstairs and see your dad."

I didn't know what to expect as I walked down those five steps into the family room. My fear of the unknown was actually worse than the reality of seeing my dad sitting in a hospital bed in the middle of our rec room, watching television while a cozy fire blazed in the fireplace.

"There's my girl," he said as I walked toward him.

We hugged like we hugged on every other of my annual visits home. Neither of us mentioned the "g-tube" that pierced his stomach or the bag attached to his intestines. In our family, we did not discuss such things.

After his initial diagnosis of cancer in July, one failed attempt at removing the tumor in August, and a series of chemotherapy treatments that ended at Thanksgiving, Dad had reconciled with his cancer. He had worked through the remorse of not dancing with his only granddaughter at her wedding, of not watching his youngest grandson graduating from high school, and of not growing old with his wife of forty-four years, my mom. The path to this evolution was now hardened ground from walking it, day in and day out, for more than five months. By the time the holiday season had arrived, his bitterness and disbelief had melded into a clean acceptance: He would cherish each precious day; he would experience each moment as a miracle of life.

Dad had lost even more weight since I'd seen him last. He had also lost much of his stamina. But he had not lost his sense of humor.

The decades-old cardboard box that held our Christmas decorations sat open on the floor near my feet. Usually, the Christmas tree was set up in the formal living room, which was used once a year for holidays. This year, the family decided to place the

Christmas tree in the rec room, because Dad could no longer climb the steps.

I retrieved the pear-shaped crocheted ornaments from the yellowed tissue paper. Although they were absolutely ugly, they'd been handmade by a long-dead aunt and hanging them on the Christmas tree was a family tradition.

"How do these ornaments look on the Christmas tree?" I asked.

My dad was in light sleep induced by the morphine dripping steadily into his veins through an intravenous port. He roused and through droopy eyes stared at the Christmas tree for several moments. At first, I thought the medicine's influence was preventing him from seeing the lighted tree . . . until he quipped, "I like 'em. They look like hooters." Then he fell into hysterical laughter at his own joke.

My mom and sisters ran down the steps to see what had caused such an outburst of laughter.

"Dad said Auntie Madge's ornaments look like hooters," I said.

We all looked at the Christmas tree, and sure enough, I had hung the two crocheted pears extremely close together. My mom, my sisters, and I joined Dad, in a fit of laughter. To some families, Dad's comment might have seemed crass on such a beloved holiday, but to this day, those faded crochet pears are referred to as the "hooter ornaments" and they still jiggle from our Christmas tree.

As Christmas Eve settled upon us, our family gathered as we had for forty-odd years, conversations booming across the room and no one stopping to really listen to the others, because we all had something to say. I watched Dad as he watched us. I cannot say whether it was his favorite Christmas, as he'd had sixty Christmases before that one. Nor can I say that it was his worst Christmas. What I can say is that I had never before seen such a look of absolute contentment on his face. Maybe surrendering to the inevitably of death enabled him to more fully appreciate the life, the laughter, and the love he had now.

Dad's composure and grace set the example for us to follow. That entire holiday, sadness never entered the room. All of us—my parents, my sisters, and I, along with my nieces, nephews, aunts, uncles, cousins, relatives many times removed, close friends, and neighbors that had not visited in years—shared in the eggnog, the camaraderie, and the bittersweet grasp that this would be Dad's final Christmas with us.

During those precious moments, I did not worry about the electric bill, the mortgage payment, or the inconsequential details that consumed my life and truly did not matter. "God Rest Ye Merry Gentlemen" played in the background, complementing the mood. The Christmas tree, a burgeoning mound of wrapped presents beneath it, lost its place as the centerpiece of the day. That honor belonged to Dad.

From his hospice bed in the center of the room, my dad reigned as the magnet that brought the family home. I realized how fortunate I was to be there. Yes, wars still raged across the globe, people still struggled and suffered every where, and my dad still had terminal cancer and was dying. Tomorrow, I would get caught up in the routines and realities of life. But on that Christmas day, for those few precious hours, the room overflowed with love and I understood what it was to know peace on earth.

—Amber Frangos

Just One

I worried that I might forget what he looked like, what he felt like. But I did not expect to be overcome with grief at the special masculine essence emanating from the chinos I was about to wash. Aftershave lotion, gasoline engines, sawdust, the hated cigarettes that took him away from us, all left a trace on his clothing. Sobbing, I rescue his work clothes from the washer, and bury my face in them, inhaling his scent.

How can I survive the loss of a husband who has been my best friend and lover for two-thirds of my life? I keen silently. *I can't do this.*

Anything can interrupt my valiant attempt to get on with my life. Tears terminate my grocery shopping when, without thinking, I reach for his favorite brand of cereal. Driving along the road, I feel the suddenly too-familiar constriction of throat, the rush of tears. *Now what brought that on?* I scold myself. It is a man walking along the road whose hair reminded me of my husband's, the handsome hair he kept to the very end.

Regaining my composure, I return the chinos to the clothes washer.

I determine that I must learn how to live alone and decide to comfort myself with a nice meal out somewhere.

I pass by his favorite restaurant, where grief once again attacks me, and so I select a new restaurant that we had never been to—a classy one.

The maitre d' approaches and asks with lifted brow, "Just one?"

My heart is wounded yet again. My eyes brimming tears, I whisper, "Just one."

My grief disables me. A friend urges me to join his widows agreement and widowers' club.

"But isn't that for people who are looking for a relationship?" I ask.

"That's the idea!" he advises.

Nope; not for me. Instead, I join an online bereavement group. It did help, at first, when I read a twenty-one-year-old's lament about losing his wife. At least I have a lifetime of memories. But then I catch the plaintive criticisms whenever a young man asks a young widow for her age.

"This is not a dating service," one harpy chides. "This is a *grief* network."

Is that what I want, to wallow in my grief? I think not, so I leave the site.

At home, I face a new problem. The liver and white Springer spaniel who has been my husband's constant companion is confused and bereft. He rebels at his loss and beleaguers me with insistent demands to be let out and in, out and in.

To add to my distress, distracted by grief, I trip over an uneven sidewalk and break my hand. In the emergency ward, my embedded wedding band is severed from my swollen finger. Another fathom to my loss.

Home from the hospital, I endure the dull pain of my hand swathed in a cast, my heart aching even more. The dog's whining crescendes into a howl. I stalk to the back door for what seems like the thousandth time to let him in. I must do something about him and this intolerable situation.

Tasting the salty tears of grief, I climb into bed and rest my throbbing hand on a pillow, the dog curled in his bed by my side. Despite the haze of pain medication, I remember the animal door I purchased a year ago that my husband had not installed.

Some time later, when my hand is comfortable, I unearth the doggy door. The directions look simple enough. *Can I do it?* I look at my cast. *It is on my left hand, and aren't I right-handed? Didn't I grow up helping in my uncle's carpentry barn?* I will try.

I search my husband's workshop lined with tools. I gather a straight edge, a pencil, and a keyhole saw and sit down on the floor next to the curious dog to measure the proposed opening. *How does one get the saw into the wood?* I dare not remove the door, as I know I can't hang it again even with two hands! *A drill. That's what I need.* Locating the drill, I rest it on my cast and bore enough holes in a row to insert the saw. But it won't cut the hard wood of the door. Through clenched teeth, I mouth a new motto, "I can DO this!" Then I drill hole after hole after hole, all around the perimeter.

I add a hammer and a chisel to my tools, and with difficulty, I manage to cut out the panel.

But wait, what is that other side? This is a hollow door with two panels? I yell swear words, and the dog leaves my side to watch from a safe distance.

"I can do this!" I mutter again, and set about drilling, chopping, and opening the other side of the door.

Admiring my work, I try to insert the doggy door. It doesn't fit. I am now screaming in anger, and the dog retreats to the bedroom.

Gritting my teeth, I again vow, "I CAN DO THIS!"

I hack away the uneven edges until I can get the contraption in. But still there is a problem. The dog door has two parts, one for each side of the door, and I have to hold both while screwing them together. Now in tears, not of grief but of frustration and desperation, I prop a chair against one side, hold the other with my cast, and fasten the assembly together.

Despite a few gouges here and there on the edges, the little door works and I have solved my first problem by myself. Somehow, in the process, my grief lifts. If I can do this, I can do anything!

I still miss my husband, I always will, but I no longer despair at being alone and helpless. "I can DO this" has become a mantra that will get me through the pangs of widowhood and lead me to a full life— even though I may remain forever a maitre d's "just one."

—*Esther Griffin*

The Way We Were

My mom and I watched movies together.
"This one is good," she'd say.

We'd sit in the dark in front of the television, taking turns brushing each other's hair while we watched the movie. Mom would smoke, and we'd drink tea and share a can of La Choy Chinese noodles. It felt criminal eating crispy noodles apart from the canned chow mein, but we did it anyway. It was our time to be bad.

Back then, I was such a good girl that being "bad" was laughable. A pudgy teen and hardworking student, I just wanted to be invisible in school. So I was startled one day when my home economics teacher, Mrs. Eveline Spruill, grabbed my arm and stuck her nose in my hair.

"You been smokin'!"

"What?" I asked.

She persisted. "You been smokin'. I smell it in your hair."

"I don't smoke!" I repeated.

"Who's been smokin' near you?"

I was bewildered. I didn't hang out with smokers. Then it dawned on me. "My mother; she smokes. We watched a movie together last night."

"Okay," she relented. "Sit down. But you smell like smoke."

Mrs. Spruill was from the South and had a thick accent. I never understood much of what she said. But I hadn't been smoking. At fourteen? At school? Me—the girl wearing a smock with ruffled sleeves and decorated with giant numbers, letters, and bicycles over a pumpkin-colored Banlon polo shirt, identical to one my (male) math teacher once wore, and a pair of Sears stretch khakis? Kids in blue jeans with button flies smoked. Not me.

Mrs. Spruill taught sewing. After the first test, "Identify the Parts of the Sewing Machine," on which I scored 100 percent, I was lost. And when she told me to put the "bawh-bin" in the machine, I was dumbfounded. I asked her to repeat the word. She did—three times. Then she spelled it: b-o-b-b-i-n. Oh. Bobbin. Put it where?

Our final project was to use our newly acquired sewing skills to make an outfit, to be worn on the last day of school. Mrs. Spruill measured me and wrote down my size. I begged to go smaller. No dice.

Mom and I ran to the fabric store. We'd spent a lot of time in fabric stores, petting bolts of corduroy, seersucker, and pique and admiring the textures, but today was different—we had an actual project to work on. Not another fantasy outfit that never got beyond the planning stage, but something I actually had to finish and then wear in mid-June.

We selected a Simplicity pattern for the jumper, an A-line with a scoop neck, and just enough royal purple, brushed-denim fabric to make the dress. Money was tight. There was no room for mistakes.

Mom and I laid the pattern out on the living room floor. On our knees with our behinds up in the air, we pinned the tissue-paper pattern to the fabric. I pulled two straight pins at a time from the tomato pincushion, storing the next pin between my teeth, like someone who really sews. Mom instantly ordered the pin removed from my mouth. What if I inhaled and the pin went down my throat? I learned that sewing together was not just stitching; it was also learning about life's small dangers at your mother's knee.

We cut the material too tight on one of the hips and had to balance it out by making a wider cut to the other hip. It looked pretty even; we were satisfied.

I brought the cut-out fabric, with the pattern still pinned to it, to school to sew. On the last day of classes, I wore the purple jumper over a white, button-down blouse. It fit okay, except at the hips, where it pulled so hard that it shimmied up my thighs and I had to keep pulling it down throughout the day. I looked around—hardly anyone else was wearing her project, not even my closest friend, who had made a lime-green sheath ("I wouldn't wear that thing!"). I looked like a fool, and felt worse. It took me thirty-three years to forgive purple, but movie nights with Mom helped in the short term.

For my mother and me, the most special movie was *The Way We Were.* It came out in theaters in 1973, and aired on the local TV channel about four years later. I was seventeen—the perfect age to share a failed romance movie with my Mom. I'd already had my first heartbreak and was taking a breather before the next one. Mom and Dad had been married for twenty years, yet she sang "Some Day My Prince Will Come" as she stood at the sink doing dishes. Robert Redford, in Navy whites, was right up our alley.

In the film, Barbra Streisand plays Katie Morosky, a Jewish political activist who falls in love with Hubbell Gardiner, played by Redford, a WASP playboy and bon vivant who is intrigued by Katie's passion for causes, a sharp contrast to the egotistical ways of the rich contemporaries who run in his circle. Naturally, the romance is doomed, because, although opposites may attract, they always end up hating each other. But also never forgetting each other. The story ends with Hubbell and his new white-bread wife running into Katie as she hands out leaflets at a "Ban the Bomb" rally. Hubbell looks at her with a love that never died and asks about their daughter. Devastating.

This is where the title song, "The Way We Were," swells and where Mom and I would cry quietly through the credits. We'd blow our noses using squares from the toilet paper roll on the coffee table. Our brushed hair was soft, like sealskin. The ashtray was full; the La Choy can was empty. Two teacups had sweet rings at the bottom.

It took me a while to figure out how someone as good-looking as Robert Redford could fall for Barbra Streisand, but even before I got it, I knew what they had was real. Mom bought the cassette tape of the music, and I often heard it playing in the years that followed, when I flew by the kitchen, running out of the house to see my friends and boyfriends between college semesters.

Well, all that smoking while watching movies and listening to music and getting teary-eyed led to emphysema for Mom twenty years later. Most of her last two years were spent sitting up in her bed, organizing pieces of ribbon, rickrack, and sewing and crafting supplies into ridiculously small boxes. Because you never know when you'll need them.

She told me, "Go on the computer and find something called 'eBay.' It's good. Lots of supplies on there. It's going to be big."

I didn't, because I didn't care about something called eBay. I was divorced and raising two boys. But I did sit with Mom on her bed, brushing her hair and she brushing mine, as we watched movies. By then, we were into *Pretty Woman*. ("It's a good one.") But still, *The Way We Were* showed up here and there.

Mom outlasted the one year of care allotted by hospice, but they kept her on anyway. She bought tickets to the circus for her aide's grandkids. She made my brothers get a dozen donuts to put at the nurses' station at the hospital when she had a breast lump removed. I protested that it was their job to help, but she insisted. She was right. It was not a bribe—it was a thank you.

Mom didn't outlast hospice forever. We knew it was coming. Fifteen minutes after we kissed her goodnight, she died while Dad sat where he'd sat since Mom got sick, in the big leather chair in the room, reading a book.

"I knew something had changed. It felt too quiet," he said. I'd lost my movie buddy, my best friend, my Mom.

In the weeks that followed, I went through Mom's things to see what to keep and what to let go of. As much as Mom was a fan of never throwing anything out, Dad called the garbage pail his "best friend." I'm with Dad, but couldn't trust him to make judgments on what was important, so I went through all her stuff. There were little boxes with mother-of-pearl button pairs and stacks of Jiffy patterns for skirts we might love in cool fabrics for the summer. One photograph showed Mom at the sewing machine. It always made my brothers and me laugh, because, although there was a lot of talk, there was almost no sewing. Mom and I were sewing wannabees, frauds even.

As I went through the boxes and bags and folders of pictures cut out from magazines ("good ideas"), I silently congratulated myself for being brave and holding up during this going-through-Mom's-stuff day. I sorted fabric swatches into piles, some on the pillow, some on my lap. Among the items, I came upon a small white box, the size of a Saltine cracker, but an inch and a half thick. It had a key. It was a music box, but plain white, the kind used inside a hand-sewn stuffed animal. I smiled. It was just like Mom to buy a music box for a bear that would never be made. I turned the key. It played "The Way We Were." I slipped the music box into my pocket.

—Christine Jelley

Family Spilling Over

I finally got the gravy boat.

For a year, I had avoided all thoughts of it because, once I got it, I'd have to accept the fact that Thelma was dead.

As long as it remained hanging on its nail in her cabin, there seemed a chance that I might go there one day to find her shuffling to the door in her slippers, a smile on her face, with a fresh story about how Katie put the run on a fox or dragged a dead muskrat up on the deck. There would be muffins in the oven, a kettle on the stove, and Thelma would bring out her best tea cups, the ones with the dainty gold filigree. She'd pour the first cup for herself and then say, as she always did, that she liked her tea weak. Katie would lie under the kitchen table twitching in doggie dreams and, when I sat in my usual chair, would put her head on my lap. I'd sip tea, relax into the rhythm of our chat, and the tension would flow out of my shoulders like mercury.

A year after Thelma's death, my husband Bill and I were invited to a family get-together at her cabin to mark the anniversary of her passing. It was to be just like the old Sunday afternoons of summer, with Thelma's grandchildren running, falling down, screaming, getting hugs and kisses, then running off again. There would be burgers and hot dogs on the fire, and we would balance on rickety chairs as we swatted mosquitoes and waved the smoke away from our faces.

But this time Thelma would not be there.

Thelma's cabin was in the bush outside Yellowknife (Northwest Territories, Canada), a little over a mile from the place that Bill and I bought the year we married—the same year Thelma's husband died, my mother died, Bill's mother got sick, and Thelma became our new family.

I had been avoiding her cabin, hadn't been there since the bright spring day a few weeks before she died when we'd gone over on our bikes and found her son gingerly helping his mother out of the truck. She was skeletal, drowning in her parka, but smiled as she lifted up her pant leg and made fun of the support hose she had to wear to help her circulation. We sat on the deck together for a few minutes, and an eagle swooped down from the sky, but Thelma was too weak to stay for long. Even then, the cabin had an unoccupied look, with weeds crawling up to the driveway and willows obscuring the view of the pond where we used to watch the ducks.

Now, I didn't want to face the emptiness of her absence. Most of all, I didn't want to face getting the gravy boat.

I'd first seen the gravy boat at one of Thelma's family dinners, in the days when she was strong and lived in the cabin alone. It was the dinner where she forgot to take the stuffing out of the turkey and nobody noticed. How we laughed about it afterward. The gravy boat had two spouts: one at the top for fat and one at the bottom for lean. I was watching my weight then, and as soon as I saw the lean juice pouring out the bottom, I knew I wanted that gravy boat.

"Hmph!" Thelma said. "You won't get it as long as I'm still alive!"

"Well, how long is that going to be?" I asked.

"You never mind!"

It became a standing joke between us. I kept trying to steal the gravy boat, but Thelma always caught me. She said she was going to live forever just so I would *never* get it. I would threaten to force her into an old-age home before her time so I could take it.

Thelma would look at me piously and say, "Let your conscience be your guide." Then she'd add, "You know where you're going when your time comes, eh?"

One day she said with a twinkle in her eye, "Show some respect for your elders. There will be a day when you come over here and find me lying dead on the floor. Then you'll be sorry."

"Well, that'll be my chance," I said. "If that happens, I'll just step over your body, take that gravy boat off the wall, and march right out of here."

We laughed. It was how we were with each other.

Then, it became serious. When Thelma got cancer the first time, when she was gaunt and crazy from her chemotherapy, she began to organize her affairs. She wrote my name in felt pen on the bottom of the gravy boat.

"When I go, come and take it," she said. "I don't know whether my kids will remember, but I want you to have it."

I didn't want the damn gravy boat anymore. I just wanted Thelma to go on living. I refused to look at it, refused to talk about it, and thought my refusal could somehow keep her alive.

She died anyway.

The barbecue to honor the anniversary of Thelma's passing was family spilling over, as much like a barbecue in the old days as it could be without Thelma there. Thelma's sister, Auntie Bertha, filled the role of matriarch. Thelma's daughters, sons, and grandchildren, including two new great-grandchildren, were there, and the chatter was familiar. Auntie Bertha brought baked beans, and the kids squealed as everybody recited over and over, "Beans, beans, the musical fruit. / The more you eat, the more you toot."

We laughed and laughed. Somewhere amidst the laughter, the screams, and the rhythms of affection, something in me let go and I began to accept Thelma's death and enjoy being at the cabin again.

Toward evening, when Bill and I were just about to leave, Thelma's daughter BJ called me into the house. I went inside, and she took the gravy boat from its nail on the wall and held it out to me. My name was still written on the bottom.

"Mom left it for you," she said. I reached out my hand. Now it was okay to have it.

—*Annelies Pool*

Gifts of Grace

When my son Eric died, he left behind letters and notes to his brother and friends, even a letter to his girlfriend's mother. For me, this beloved younger son left a short line of words scribbled just before he left life.

"I love you, Mom," he had written with a shaky hand.

Those words meant so much. Yet, somehow, I felt left out, jealous of Eric's friends to whom he had managed to write long pages.

In those first sorrow-washed weeks and months after his death, I clung precariously to the faith I had previously taken for granted. No other loss or struggle had so tested my mental balance. Emotion-ally, I was on overload even before Eric's unexpected death. In less than three years, five family members had died, including my parents. Further, I was in culture shock from retiring and moving across the country to California. Further complicating my life were fresh knee injuries not healing well.

I had been only a few months in my new home when this last blow descended, the worst that a parent can know. After Eric's funeral in our home state of Texas, I stayed on for a few weeks with my older son, Andrew. But as soon as Eric's affairs were settled, Andrew returned to the demands of graduate school and his job. It was not easy for him, either, as my sons had been very close. But I returned to California knowing that Andrew had a strong support system of friends.

During the next critical months, my new neighbors—some of whom I scarcely knew—and the minister of the church I now attended offered me kind support. What I missed most was someone to talk with who had known me as part of a large, happy family, someone with whom to share memories of Eric.

My doctor offered me sleeping pills for grief-haunted nights. I declined. He suggested grief counseling, and I established weekly counseling sessions with both my minister and a psychiatrist.

The faith that had sustained me during those earlier, more natural deaths was shaky now as I tried to come to terms with the unnatural sequence of losing my son. Like all parents who have lost a child, I asked the agonizing question, "Why, God?" I prayed for understanding. Counseling helped me to understand the grief process. My doctor directed me to Compassionate Friends, a national organization of parents who have lost children. I hesitated at first to attend a meeting, but once I met other parents who were living through my kind of loss, I saw that survival was possible. During the first weeks of initial shock and when the finality of Eric's death hit home, I had not been sure of that.

One sleepless night, I opened a box of Eric's things that I had brought back from Texas. Among them were several diaries written in his crabbed handwriting, from all the way back to his early teens. I had not known he kept journals. With the handwriting so difficult to decipher, I decided to type them out for his brother to read later.

Keeping busy with this project, along with restoring the neglected garden and old house I had bought, I ignored the calendar's progression into the holiday season. All I wanted of Christmas was the impossible: for God to turn back the clock and restore my precious son to me.

On a rainy mid-December morning when I was unable to work in the garden, I opened a diary Eric had kept during his fourteenth year. He had been a private person, a quiet boy. He had loved baseball, motors of all kinds, and music. On the cusp between boyhood and manhood, he was miserable that year. His father and I had divorced the year before. Mononucleosis with persistent fever had kept him confined to bed for months. In his diary, he had written down all the anger and frustration that he had not been able to express aloud, even to his brother.

As I typed his words, my tears fell on the keyboard. The teen years are seldom easy for anyone. That we, his family, had not understood the depth of Eric's unhappiness was almost unbearable to learn now that he was gone. Soon, I was sobbing until I thought my heart would literally break. Grief overwhelmed me.

Hours passed. I knew, finally, that I must find a way to stop crying before I got sick. I owed it to Andrew to try. I plunged into housework. Still, it was hard to stop thinking about Eric. Worst of all, the last page I typed had expressed anger at me. Eric had wanted to attend a ballgame, and I had kept him home because he still had a low-grade fever. I was following doctor's orders, but the boy's anger was directed at me. It hurt to read that, despite the years that had passed since the incident.

"Why didn't he leave me a letter, too?" I cried out. "If I could just speak with him one more time, hear his voice once more." Just then the doorbell rang. When I answered, there stood my next-door neighbor, Ann, with a freshly baked coffee cake.

"May I come in?" she asked, closing her umbrella. "If you've got coffee, I've got cake just out of the oven."

Although we had spoken only in passing before Eric's death, she had offered friendship and help afterward, and we had become close. Now, she could see I had been crying, and she matter-of-factly came in and set her offering on the kitchen table.

"I think you need a break. I do. Where are your plates?" she continued, bustling about.

I put the kettle on to heat water for instant coffee and got out mugs. Then I realized my napkins and small plates were as yet unpacked. My spare bedroom was still filled with unopened trunks and boxes.

"Just a minute. I think I know where my dishes are. I've been using just one plate while I work on the house," I told her and went to look.

Shoving a small footlocker aside to get to a dish barrel, there on the floor sticking partway out from under a box, lay a scrap of paper. It was so small that I almost left it to be gobbled up later by the vacuum cleaner. But something made me lean over to pick it up. As I started to crumple it, I recognized Eric's handwriting on one side. It was a tiny note that said, "I love you, Mom."

I stood very still, scarcely breathing. Logic told me that this scrap of paper must have been one of many such notes from Eric that I had received over the years. Small love notes are a custom in our family. My heart told me this was a gift that had come when I most needed it. It was tangible solace, words that I could hold in my hand, to read and to touch again and again. Yet, how had the note come to be here? Eric had never visited me in this house. But I did not question it.

"Thank you, God," I whispered.

I had planned to hide from Christmas that year. But Christmas had come to me in the gift of a neighbor's caring friendship and in a gift of words from my son that said all I needed to hear. "I love you, Mom." He had said it to me in life and he said it again now on a scrap of paper. What lengthy letter from Eric could have said more that mattered?

How clearly it came to me that day that, no matter how painful our circumstances, if we hold tightly to faith, keeping ourselves open to receiving gifts of grace, those gifts do come. Love is the undying connection, both human and divine.

—Marcia E. Brown

The Ring

The misty winter darkness brings on a dim, comforting cloak of sheltering invisibility. I've grown used to being invisible since he died and my entire life suddenly became an unknown, no longer even vaguely familiar stranger to me. Demanding that I accommodate her, this stranger nags at me, calls to me, until eventually I seek her, long for her, allow her to possess me. Her insistence distracts me from the one thought that never leaves me, the one certainty left to me. Her ceaseless demands allow me to occasionally forget, for just a moment or maybe for a short string of moments, that he is dead and far away and that I am dead and still here, trying to pretend a different life.

Sometimes I wonder if he would recognize me if, unexpectedly, I entered a room he was in or walked past a window he was gazing through. I'll never forget the beauty of him—his dark, melancholy eyes, his easy smile, the long stride of his walk, the sound of his voice saying my name, his deep hearty laugh. But would he remember me?

Little about me has changed since he died. Maybe my eyes are weary and sad now, but they are still green. My smile is not as bright as when I smiled at him, but I still smile sometimes. My dark auburn hair is not quite as rich as it was when he loved it blowing free, but it's still the same hair falling loose at my shoulders. I'm still as tall as I was when we walked hand-in-hand, nearly shoulder-to-shoulder, together. Surely he would recognize me?

I like this brief period between early evening and starlight that helps mark the close of another day I've managed to endure, which is what I do now. And I do it remarkably well, considering how I long for him every hour of every day of every month for so many seemingly endless years. I don't wonder how or why this became my life. It just did, because having such a large hole through my heart allows me, at best, merely half a life, and usually I'm content with this. Only when that half threatens to become less do I seek out a church, hoping to discover him in there, waiting for me.

So many times I've looked for him in a church, wherever in the world I've wandered to, only to find it empty of this man of God I still love so much. It is not surprising I am here in Old Heidelberg, in old Europe, where the streets are narrow and not a soul recognizes me, making it easy to disappear. Aimlessly following the walkway along the dark side of the cathedral, in the neighborhood of the third university established by the Holy Roman Empire, I wonder if I should enter, on the chance he might be in there waiting for me.

Walking along the pathway, I'm glad the day is ending. The shiny, wet cobblestones underfoot demand I watch my step, but weary and lost in thought, I'm not really paying attention to where I'm going when, to my left, something catches my eye. I stop for a moment, looking toward a tiny, dancing light begging for recognition by moving in perfect synchrony with my heartbeat. I dart through the foot traffic, pulled into this mysterious flicker as a moth is drawn to a flame, growing more intense the closer it comes. I am astonished to find its source is a gold ring barely visible through the wavy glass shop window, dim with grime. I stop to look.

"*Rote gold*," the old shopkeeper tells me from the doorway. "Very unusual," he adds, switching to English.

He's right, red gold is rare.

"*Alte*," he tells me. "*Sehr alte.*"

"Of course it is," I say. "This is an antique store; everything here is very old."

"*Ja*," he says agreeably. "You want to see it?"

"*Ja*," I nod, having no idea how he knows what piece of jewelry has been so brazenly demanding my attention.

"Try it?" he asks, handing me the ring.

"*Ja*," I say.

I find that this shiny gold band bearing the twelve zodiac signs encircled around it fits both my ring fingers, which I thought were different sizes, perfectly. I've never seen a ring so unusual, and if I'd ever had the chance to choose a wedding ring, it would've been this one. I always wanted my wedding ring to be rose gold, but knowing there will never be that wedding, it's not something I think about anymore.

"Unusual," I say.

"*Ja*," the old man says.

"Who wore such a ring?" I ask.

"A church rector," he explains, nodding toward the cathedral street, where, only moments ago, I was aimlessly wandering.

"The zodiac is an imaginary pathway around the heavens—a place of great interest to the early church," he explains with a chuckle. "*Ist der ring—es gut?*" he asks, nodding toward the ring.

"*Ja—ist es gut,*" I say. "It's very good," I whisper, wondering why the ring, if it is what he claims, is not in the possession of the church?

"Ten Deutsch marks, including the certificate," he says.

I expected one hundred times this price, and being surprised he asks so little, I don't respond. I notice the tag he removed before handing the ring to me says DM 850. He notes my puzzlement.

"It has been waiting for you to find it," he says matter-of-factly, intently looking at me from behind round glasses.

I remain quiet.

"This ring belongs to you. Someone intends for you to have it, has been waiting for you to find it," he repeats.

"I'm ten thousand miles from home, in a place I've never been, and you are asking me to believe this ring has been waiting here for me to find it?"

My question perplexes him. "It fits you on both hands; this is unusual. It means the ring is yours, you just didn't know it until now," he says evenly, again looking directly at me in a way that makes me want to believe him more than to doubt what he is telling me. He is offering to sell me the ring for eighty-five times less than its apparent value, and unless it's extremely overpriced, this makes no sense.

"The certificate—may I see it?"

He hands me a yellowed piece of paper. Despite my sparse German, I am able to decipher documentation that the ring is what he says it is and dated in the late eighteenth century.

"Why isn't this in a museum?"

"Rings having zodiac symbols are rare but not extremely so, and some were used, often by Jews, as marriage rings—to signify marriage as a heavenly, perhaps holy, state. If a church museum thinks a ring has a marriage history, it doesn't want it," he explains.

"Does this ring have that history?" I ask.

"*Ja*—probably. Otherwise the church would have it." He smiles. "They either buried the ring with the priest who wore it or took it off at death and passed it on to another one."

"How would a ring change from belonging to a priest to becoming a symbol of marriage?"

"The priest might give it to someone—a friend, perhaps. There was no confusion, because priests wore the rings on their left hand, to show marriage to the church or maybe to God, and the Jews wore their marriage rings on the right hand, because they, more sensibly, marry real people." He smiles again— the twinkle in his eyes revealing a patient kindness that says he doesn't have to sell me this ring, but he wants me to have it.

"Or the priest could marry and just move the ring to the other hand," I offer.

"*Ja*, that too," he agrees.

I am silent, trying to decipher the sign on the door behind him. I think it says the store is closed on Mondays and Tuesdays, and also on Wednesdays in winter, and never open past four in the afternoon on any day. It is half past five on a January Monday.

"You aren't usually open now. Why are you here this evening?" I ask.

"In case the owner would come for the ring today; it was important to be here," he says assuredly.

"And you think I am that person?" I ask.

"*Ja*," he nods again.

"And if I pay you DM10, the ring is mine?"

"*Ja*, but I will take less. I cannot keep something that doesn't belong to me after the person who is supposed to have it appears," he says.

"The ring costs more. How about if I give you DM20?" I ask, looking him in the eye.

Looking back at me, he shakes his head no, saying this is too much, that DM10 is the right price.

I hand him DM10; he hands me the certificate, wishes me "*Guten abend*," and locks the door behind me. When I look back a moment later, the shop is dark.

Later that evening, sitting in a small bistro having a glass of wine, I struggle to understand what just happened to me that led me to be wearing a rose gold ring on my right hand. This is the same hand upon which I'd previously worn a thin platinum ring of encircled hearts given to me by the man I grieve—the one whose leaving shot a cannon through my still young heart. That ring spontaneously broke into pieces mere hours before I learned of the accident . . . split apart at perhaps the precise moment of his death.

Weeks later, several jewelers told me the ring was beyond repair. "So is my heart," I always responded. Eventually, without knowing why, I surrendered the broken ring to the river that had claimed the life of the man who had placed it upon my finger, knowing that giving it up would leave me truly empty-handed.

My love's abrupt departure from my life left me with so many unanswered questions. All the things we never got around to saying itch worse than rough wool against bare skin. In the language of his world, these unsaid words are my hair shirt and I wear it uneasily.

Could it be this ring a stranger insists belongs to me is answering the persistent questions that have haunted me for so long? Is it irrefutable evidence of life beyond the grave, absolute proof that those we truly love and who truly love us in return never really leave us? Is this man I've loved in life and in death, across time and eternity, saying he's still here? Is the German shopkeeper in this place half a world away from home his messenger? Was I drawn here, to a foreign place I've never visited before, to find this stranger who has given voice to the spirit of the man I love, whose own voice is unable to be heard? Is dead, like alive, simply another way of being in the world?

Absent any other explanation for an otherwise entirely unexplainable encounter, I finally conclude the answer to all of these questions is yes. But it is an uneasy answer—demanding a faith in the unseen and unknowable that only by grace alone will I be able to abide.

—Paula v.Wende Dáil

Paying Homage

I was getting nowhere. Mom and I were carrying on a duplicate conversation of one we'd had last year—and the year before that. She insisted on driving from Brainerd to Minneapolis on Memorial Day to place red geraniums on her husband's grave. I tried to talk her out of it.

"I'll be fine. I'll stop at McDonald's on my way home, use the rest room and get coffee and a twist cone. McDonald's has wonderful coffee." My mother, the Swedish java aficionado.

"Mom, now that Larry's gone, don't you think he realizes that all this driving just to put flowers at the cemetery is foolish? He's not really there."

I'd gone too far.

"No, dear. The last time we made the trip to put red geraniums at his sister's grave, we promised if anything happened to either of us, the one left would continue the tradition. Case closed."

She said a quick goodbye, and I said a quick prayer that she'd be safe.

That last Memorial Day of her life, Mom zipped down to Sunset Memorial Gardens in her blue Oldsmobile to pay tribute to her dead husband and his sister. I can see her as if I had been there. So small that only her curly white hair was visible, she looked like a Q-tip behind the steering wheel. In the trunk, organized in a cardboard box, would be a brown straw whisk broom, a small gardening shovel, and a pair of scissors. Inside the armrest she'd have candy-coated peanuts and butterscotch candies. "Just in case."

She'd be wearing Liz Claiborne jeans with an elastic waistband, her sweatshirt with red, white, and blue American flags embroidered across the front, and white Ked's tennies. Inside the left cuff of her sweatshirt would be a hankie. "Just in case."

She'd clip the dead grass around the grave, whisk it into a pile with her hand-held broom, and make an edging around the stone. She'd plant red geraniums in green tin vases with sharp-pointed bottoms and stick them into the ground at the top of the stones. After she finished, she'd gather the clippings into a baggie.

I see all this because I accompanied her on the first two Memorial Days after my stepfather died. After that, I wasn't allowed back. Maybe I didn't take it seriously enough.

Memorial Day was sacred to our family. Every year, our parents took the five of us children from Minneapolis to St. Peter to put flowers on the graves of my mother's parents. Both had died before I was born.

After being cooped up in the car, we eagerly scrambled to the grave site, running between the headstones. "I think it's this way" was followed by, "No, it's over there," before we ended up at the right place. Mom knelt first, then Dad, followed by the five of us kids. I never knew what to say to these strangers buried beneath the Elmquist stone.

Years later, after Dad's parents died, we stopped in St. Paul on the way back from St. Peter to put flowers on their graves. I was thirteen and felt foolish kneeling on the prickly grass. Should I pray to God? Nana and Papa? I clasped my hands, bent my head, and moved my lips.

Three years later, my parents were divorced. Our traveling cemetery-show ended.

I remember telling Mom after Dad died that I put flowers on his grave for Memorial Day.

"Why waste your time? He thought it was stupid," she said.

"What about all the years we went to St. Peter and Resurrection? Dad went."

"Unwillingly."

I don't care. I like going. The headstones at Fort Snelling, a cemetery for those who served their country, stand upright, row after row, like soldiers at attention. Dad is laid to rest over the hill from an airport runway. He loved flying, and I picture him sitting on the headstone, watching planes take off and land.

When Mom passed away from a heart attack, it happened so fast I never got to say goodbye. We drove to Brainerd twice that week—once to make funeral arrangements and again for the memorial service.

"It's not that long a drive," my husband said. "Why didn't we make it more often?"

"It seemed farther."

We cleaned out Mom's car and found the cardboard box with the cemetery tools in the trunk. I knew how I could thank her and stay in touch. "I'll keep those," I told my husband.

"I'll put them in the trunk of your car," he said. "And put some of her candy in your glove box. Just in case."

The Memorial Day tradition falls to me, the oldest. I'm happy with that. It's my way of saying everything I would have said in the hospital. When I buy the red geraniums and head to the cemeteries, the box of tools rattling in the trunk, I'm saying, "I love you."

Last year, I called my sister. "I'm going to the cemeteries tomorrow. Want to go with me?"

"She's not there, you know."

"I know."

"Why go then?"

"It was important to Mom."

What I really wanted to tell her was that, as second oldest, she'll need to carry on when I'm gone.

Our conversation was still bouncing around in my head as I brushed the dead grass from the grave marker the next day. I stuffed the geranium into the metal cone, stabbed the pointed end into the ground, and added an American flag.

I looked up and noticed a small woman, about eighty, kneeling on the ground not far from me. Her white head was bent as she clipped the grass away from a headstone. Next to her was a container holding a single red flower and a box with a yellow whisk broom and a small shovel. She wore jeans, a white sweatshirt with an American flag on the front, and tennis shoes. Pausing, she wiped her face with the back of her hand, then pulled a Kleenex from her sleeve. *You're wrong*, I silently told my sister. *She is here. She's everywhere.*

—*Andrea Langworthy*

This story was first published on BoomerWomen Speak.com.

Carolina Blue

It's a month after my father's funeral, and I have been floundering in an intensive writing course for weeks. I don't mean to be difficult; it's just that I have no words. Empty, I write meaningless prose in rote response to assignments. I save nothing because nothing is worth saving. I write on scrap paper and throw it away. I scribble on napkins and give them to strangers. I am writing into a void.

Today, we are on a writing marathon, walking the streets of Charleston, stopping here, stopping there, recording images—like collecting photographs for an album that isn't mine. I fill pages with observations of what is outside of me—carefully distanced, carefully controlled. What is inside of me stays there, tense and tight. As we tramp along, we pass a woman with dragons covering her arms, smoking a cigarette outside a tattoo shop.

A fellow student, Tracey, says, "Tattoos are symbols, like words, and they carry meaning."

Our group leader, Tom, adds, "Perhaps we say things with tattoos that we can't say other ways."

I touch the black cord I tied around my wrist on the day my father died. I know about symbols.

Tom sees my gesture. He says, "If you can't write it on paper, maybe you can write it on your body."

I smile on the inside and outside for the first time in a month. The whole group agrees to write about me getting a tattoo, and we head to the parlor.

I first saw my father's tattoos the weekend before he started radiation treatment. Blue, like a child's crayon drawings, they spread across his chest, marking him for the radiologist's aim. Trying to kill the cancer that was stopping his breath, the doctors burned him. His voice was rough and he could barely eat, barely drink the high-calorie smoothies my stepmother made for him. For weeks, he returned for more burning. After treatment, he showed off his tattoos like battle scars.

They didn't save him.

At his funeral, the University of North Carolina basketball program came out in force. Players and former players I knew and others I didn't know towered over the rest of the packed church. My father,

Jim Hudock, was Dean Smith's first team captain in the 1961–62 season. The players and coaches I knew passed out blue and white buttons showing the UNC logo and "33"—my dad's number. Others I didn't know introduced themselves in soft tones as they picked up buttons, small in their large hands. We all put them on, the blue "UNC 33" making visible one of my father's greatest loves.

When I was growing up, I watched my dad play ball like a madman. On the court, he would push himself, push around others, and top everyone else in his need to win. But when he walked off the court, he and his opponents went to get a beer together.

He taught me the same lesson at the dinner table. We would debate issues, politics, and opinions with warmth and feeling. He never personally attacked and always kept the discussion in the realm of intellectual debate. When it was all over, he would hug me and say, "I like the way you stand up for your beliefs, even when they are different than mine."

He was the first Republican in generations of our family; I was a liberal Democrat. He complained about welfare freeloaders and entitlement programs; I wanted universal health care. He hated Bill Clinton more than anything else I can imagine; I worked to get him elected. We reflected the red state/blue state split right there in our house, and we loved to do battle for our team.

On one of my visits home from graduate school during Bill Clinton's first campaign, I heard on the radio that Clinton was coming through the Kinston airport—at 3:00 A.M. The night was cold; it was less than a week until the election and fall had settled in well. Not a night owl nor a person who likes the cold, I decided to force myself to get up and go shake the big man's hand anyway. I'd heard him speak before, but this would be a small enough group to see him up close. I felt the turn in the campaign, and I knew I would be shaking the hand of a man soon to become President. The alarm woke me, I got out of bed, and there was my dad, standing in the hall, fully dressed. He'd been waiting for me.

"You know, I don't like him. But I like that you believe enough in someone that you'll get up at this time of the morning and go stand at a cold airport." He pulled me close. "I'm proud of you."

Basketball taught my father how to fight to win but also how to respect his opponents. He passed that along to me. And I became a teacher and a professor and a writer whose life is spent in the arena of intellectual combat. He helped make me who I am.

Who and what we love marks us. Ancient tribes marked themselves to show they belonged; warriors displayed their scars to remember what was lost and what was won; mothers cut themselves to reveal a child had died. To some, tattooing is a rite of passage, of moving from one state of existence to another, of growing up, of becoming an adult. As a now fatherless daughter, I, too, am moving into a new way of being, a new kind of adult. So it is right that I will now mark myself with the symbol from those buttons we wore at the funeral. I want to make that mark permanent. So I always remember. So what he loved is imprinted on me. So I can see part of him every day.

The tattoo artist, Tim, yells to signal my turn, "Get in here, Tarheel."

I feel that what he says is right and true. I am also Carolina blue. Because I was born in Chapel Hill. Because I later returned to get my first degree. Because I am my father's daughter.

I let the tattoo form. I feel each movement of the pen throughout my body, the pain bringing me into shape. The UNC logo. The number 33. A tattoo my father would have wanted—rather than the one he got.

—*Amy Hudock*

Burying Bea

It is tradition in my family to dig the grave for the newly departed—a bizarre tradition, but tradition nonetheless. The passing of a loved one can be a difficult time for the family, and funerals are generally filled with sorrow. Years ago, my family decided to honor our dearly departed with a celebration of sorts, which is how the tradition of grave digging began. Laughter was the sole reason for this ritual.

As I climbed the sloping hill behind Blackburn Church, a wave of sadness swept over me as I imagined my grandparents' wedding many years ago at that same sanctuary. I'd never asked Grandma Bea about that day. We'd never discussed her hopes and dreams, even though she had always been supportive of mine. Guilt mixed with sorrow as I chastised myself once again for not waking my grandmother on one of the last days of her life. I'd missed my chance to say goodbye, to tell her I loved her.

The holiday season can be overwhelming and that Christmas had been no exception. Hurrying into my grandmother's room at the nursing home to deliver her annual gift of See's candy, I'd found her sleeping. Her roommate was also sleeping, and I struggled with the decision of whether to wake my grandmother. I knew that if I did, she'd experience temporary confusion as to who I was. At my previous visits, she'd eventually make the connection, a smile lighting up her face as she said my name. But I was in a hurry. Did I really want to wake her, only to have her not know who I was and risk not having the time to stay until that smile of recognition lit her face? I left quietly, not knowing that the image of my sleeping grandmother would be my last memory of her.

At the top of the hill, we Thompson women stood hunched against the cold January wind, our voices and laughter carried away with each frosty breath as we contemplated the frozen Oklahoma dirt.

I am the oldest of Mutt and Bea's grandchildren and, in my opinion, the most like Grandma Bea. My grandmother and I loved a good story. She had dabbled in writing throughout the years, creating wonderful poetry, touching short stories, and much-anticipated family letters.

Months after her passing, I came across a short story that she'd written in 1970 as a tribute to a fir tree she could see from her hospital room, where she was recovering from gallbladder surgery. She'd penned it when I was in junior high school and the world was in turmoil. My grandmother had paid homage to the fir tree, painting a picture of a tiny seedling struggling to survive the elements to reach maturity. She imagined what stories the tree itself would tell if it could speak. The last paragraph of my grandmother's story echoed in my mind each time I felt myself navigating a difficult time.

"If we would examine our hearts and minds, plant our feet firmly on the ground like this ageless fir tree, and lift our eyes and hearts toward the heavens, we would know that the turmoil of our present day shall become the history of our tomorrow."

My grandmother's love for storytelling is how we came to be at Blackburn Church. She would be buried in the church's small cemetery. Her funeral service, to be held the next day, would be a celebration of her life as those who loved her encircled her final resting place and shared their favorite Bea stories.

"I think the ground's too frozen to dig," my cousin Mandi said.

"God, I hope not." I stepped into the family circle and toed the ground.

Handing me a steaming mug, my sister Lori said, "Maybe if we toast the dirt, the dig will be easier."

We hoisted our hot toddies in salute to the cold, hard Oklahoma soil . . . and, of course, to Beatrice Thompson, mother of five, grandmother to nine.

My cousin Rita Lee, who's named after my mother, grabbed the shovel and asked, "Who wants to dig first?"

"Wait," Lori said. "Let's take pictures first."

My sister took the shovel from Rita Lee and struck a pose.

We finished the photo shoot and took turns digging the hole. Lori placed the urn into the small opening and put a couple of Grandma's favorite peppermint candies on top as she said goodbye. We each took a turn adding a handful of dirt as we said our silent farewells. The wind had picked up, and dark clouds swirled across the waning sun, causing the temperature to drop from frosty to freezing.

I cast a worried glance at the sky. "Mom, did you make arrangements to hold the service inside if the weather turns bad?"

"No." She blinked at me from behind her bifocals. "Do you think we should?"

"It might be a good idea."

Six sets of eyes looked up at the darkening sky.

"Kimila, would you speak with Pastor Dave?" Aunt Glenda asked. "You're good at arranging things."

"Sure," I said. "I'll see what I can do."

I trudged toward the church and found Pastor Dave in his office. After I explained my predicament, he escorted me to his secretary, Kathy.

"Kathy," Pastor Dave said, "this is Kimila. She and her family are preparing the grave for her grandmother, and—"

"They're doing what?" Kathy stood abruptly, sending her chair careening into the wall behind her.

"Uh, we're digging the hole for my grandmother's ashes." My stomach clenched at the look of incredulity and anger on Kathy's face.

"Who gave you permission to do such a thing?" Kathy asked, hands on hips.

"I'm . . . not sure. I believe my mother and aunt spoke with someone and made arrangements."

"Well, they didn't talk to me!" Kathy narrowed her eyes at me, then turned to Pastor Dave. "I'll take care of this, sir," she said with a tight smile.

Pastor Dave nodded, looking relieved that he hadn't given permission to dig the hole.

"Come on," Kathy said. "I need to talk to your family."

Boisterous laughter reached us before we crested the first hill. When my family came into view, I knew instantly that they were in the middle of another toast.

I waved and called out, "I found someone who can help."

A frenzy of activity muted their laughter, and I assumed they were hiding the thermos of hot toddies. We were at a church, after all, and coffee laced with a little schnapps might be perceived as disrespectful.

"Mom, Aunt Glenda, this is Kathy," I said. "She's in charge of funeral services for the church. She'd like to know who you spoke with regarding digging Grandma's . . . hole."

"Let's see . . ." My mother put a finger to her chin. "It was, uh, do you remember who you spoke with, Glenda?"

"Me?" My aunt glared at my mother. "You said you'd make all the arrangements."

"Well, I left a message for someone . . ." A pink hue colored my mother's cheeks.

"Is there a problem with us digging the hole for our grandmother's ashes?" Lori asked.

"Possibly," Kathy said, hands on hips once again. "You see, we have two William Thompsons. You might have the wrong gravesite."

"Well, I'm guessing you don't have two William *Mutt* Thompsons," Rita Lee said, pointing to the headstone, which declared that William Mutt Thompson had been laid to rest in 1986. Grandma Bea's name had been etched next to his.

Kathy looked at the large gravestone and said in a sarcastic tone, "Yes, well, there's still one problem."

"What's that?" Mandi asked, mimicking Kathy's hands-on-hips stance.

"You've dug the hole on the wrong side of the gravestone." Kathy crossed her arms.

All eyes glanced at the small mound of earth at the bottom of the stone, where my grandmother's ashes now lay. I swear I could hear Grandma Bea laughing.

"In our cemetery, the deceased are buried with footstones, not headstones," Kathy said. "Your grandparents' gravestone was placed at the foot of your grandfather's casket. You've placed Mrs. Thompson in someone else's plot."

"Oh," we said in unison.

Our laughter bubbled up like a leak in a damn, and then burst forth in a full roar. Tears streamed down our cheeks, and my mother and aunt crossed their legs in an effort not to wet themselves.

"Well, we . . . we can fix it." Lori grabbed the shovel and stifled another giggle.

"If that's okay," Rita Lee said, a grin splitting her face.

"Fine," Kathy said. "But please make sure the ground doesn't look disturbed."

"Yes, of course." Mandi nodded her agreement.

"Um, Kathy," I said. "If the weather isn't cooperative tomorrow, can we hold the service inside the church?"

"I'm sure the weather will hold," Kathy said, turning toward the church. "If not, I'll see what I can do."

"Thanks," I said to her retreating back.

"I'm sorry, honey," my mother said. "I really didn't think digging the hole would be a problem."

Lori and Rita Lee removed Grandma Bea from the wrong side of the gravestone, while Mandi and I dug a new hole. As we tidied the area, I wondered if my brothers and uncle, who were still enroute, would have known about the positioning of the gravestone. I smiled as I imagined their reaction to our tale of two holes. Thank God we'd only been responsible for burying Bea's urn . . . and not a coffin.

The January wind howled around us, sucking the warmth from our bodies. Gathered around the new hole, we were silent except for chattering teeth. Lori held Grandma Bea's ashes in shaking hands and placed the urn gently back into the ground.

"Goodbye again, Grandma," she said.

This time I placed six new pennies, face up on top of the urn, remembering one of my grandmother's favorite quotes: "See a penny pick it up; someday it will bring you luck."

Once again, we each took a turn filling in the hole, repeating our goodbyes.

"I think we should sing before we go," Rita Lee said.

"It's cold," Glenda said. "Let's go home."

"We've got time for one song, Mama," Mandi said. "What do you want to sing, Rita Lee?"

"'Amazing Grace,'" she said. "Kimila, do you have the lyrics with you?"

"I do." I pulled a wrinkled piece of paper from my coat pocket.

Everyone gathered around as I held the paper tightly to keep it from blowing away. We broke out in song, but before we finished the first verse, a voice boomed from the bottom of the hill.

"For God's sake, stop singing!" When Hollie, Rita Lee's daughter, reached the top of the hill, she hugged each of us. "It's a good thing great-grandma's dead; y'all are ruining her favorite song."

"Will you sing for us?" Rita Lee asked.

"That's why I came," Hollie said with a smile. "I was afraid that if you tried to sing, the church would ban you from coming to the service tomorrow."

We were now three generations of Thompson women saying goodbye to Bea, who had come full circle. Her final journey—as ashes in a carry-on bag from Oregon to Oklahoma, to her proper resting place at Blackburn Church—would prove to be a well-told story over the next few years.

As the blustery wind carried Hollie's voice toward heaven, I knew that my grandmother would have loved that this story would be her last. She would have found comfort in our efforts to carry on tradition and humor at our ineptness in doing so.

As was the case with the fir tree in her story many years earlier, while Beatrice Thompson had not led a simple life, she had withstood raging elements with her feet firmly planted on the ground, faith filling her heart, and her eyes looking toward heaven—where she knew God waited for her.

—*Kimila Kay*

In My Own Time

"Will it ever stop hurting?" I ask, leaning against the wall in the narrow hallway, as if it might soak up some of my sorrow.

Reluctant to face the darkness outside alone, I am the last of the group to emerge from the small meeting room. Rachel, the group facilitator, gathers her raincoat and keys and prepares to lock up the Grief and Loss Center for the night. After three hours of describing my own despair and listening to the other women express the rawness of their pain, I feel spent. Yet, as I walk toward the door, more tears spring from some unstoppable source, forging new trails down my damp cheeks.

Rachel touches my shoulder and says with a quiet certainty, "At some point, Laurie, you'll realize that there are other things you would rather be doing on a Monday night."

"I can't even imagine it," I whisper, even while I cling to the possibility that she is right. I wrap my coat tightly around my thin, run-down body and head back into the world of which I no longer feel a part. A world that doesn't seem to notice or care that I have lost the person closest to me on the planet and that I'm not sure that I can bear it.

A sharp wind blows the last of autumn's leaves in senseless swirls; they scuttle and scurry haphazardly through the empty streets. Caught against curbs, they flap pointlessly or fall, brittle and used, into the grates of corner gutters. The wipers on my car swish quickly back and forth across the windshield, keeping time with the pelting rain, working hard to keep the glass clear so I can make my way back home. But there is no home to go to anymore. Not since that black July night when I watched my mother die in the back bedroom, while all the neighbors slept safely in their beds.

My mother walked three miles a day, rarely had so much as a cold, and seemed destined for the same centenarian status that her mother and aunts had achieved. But a lemon-sized tumor that had silently infiltrated the front right lobe of her brain had plans of its own. Eagerly, it stretched its cancer-filled tentacles into the far reaches of my mother's brain, stealing life from her, one faculty at a time.

I fly home and move back into the childhood bedroom that I'd left ten years before. For the next two years, I rarely leave my mother's side—through brain surgeries and countless seizures, after she stops walking and talking, during the months of open-eyed coma. And when, just after sunrise on that summer morning, I watch the black van carrying my mother's body drive up and over the hill and I see the neighbor step out on his porch in his pajamas to get the paper and unroll it to read the headlines, I've never felt so utterly bereft.

"So what are you going to do now?" my mother's friend asks with an upbeat tone in the church hall as she folds up the program from the memorial service, the one with the photo of a field of daisies on it, and stuffs it away in her purse. "Now you can finally get on with your own life," she adds, searching my face for a spark, a smile, something to show her that I am "fine" and ready to "join the living," some cue to make her feel better.

Over the next few months, I am bombarded with similar comments:

"At least she is out of her suffering."

"It is God's will."

"Your mother wouldn't want to see you wallow." . . .

A few friends seem to understand the depth of my despair. But most people seem to think that the hard part is over now that my mother has died. I feel pressured to pack up my feelings into a little box, tie it with a tidy bow, and set it aside to collect dust like any other souvenir from my past.

After months of feeling like an alien, one who apparently doesn't "do grief" well, I find a tattered, gray business card in the pocket of a sweater stashed in the trunk of my car. A woman I'd met briefly at Nordstrom's, where I was returning a skirt my mother had bought and never had the chance to wear, handed it to me after I'd started crying at the counter. Lost in my fog, I'd forgotten about it.

I call the number. Perhaps there is a place to find some solace, after all.

The following Monday evening, I am one of six women who tentatively form a circle around a blue pillar candle and a box of tissues. Given how men and women process their emotions differently, Rachel doesn't lead co-ed groups.

"Most people in our culture deny their grief," she says. "A few days or weeks to feel sad is considered socially acceptable, and then we are expected to snap back to "normal," as though nothing has happened. We aren't taught that grieving is a natural part of life, that feelings of loss are to be honored, and that, yes, it takes time."

Rachel's words soothe like an elixir for which I have been starved.

"When you listen to each other's stories, try not to judge your pain or loss as being worse than another's," she warns.

Slowly, the room becomes animated as each woman shares how her life has been affected by death. One woman's husband of thirty years died of a heart attack—on the treadmill she had just given him for his birthday. Another has lost her twin sister—murdered. One woman grieves for the childhood she was denied at the hands of her abusive father. A woman's three-year-old daughter awoke with a fever and was dead by the time help arrived. One woman's cat has died.

At first, I stumble from meeting to meeting. As I go through the motions of living the remainder of the week, I try to wear the mask of one who has now healed from her grief. Usually, by Friday, I am just hanging on until Monday night. With these women in this little room, amidst tears and occasional episodes of aching laughter, it is the only time all week that I feel free to admit my lingering anguish.

We develop a camaraderie born of a pain that we each yearn to move beyond. Gently, Rachel guides us through the uncharted terrain, reminding us over and over again that with grief "the only way out is through."

She explains that hiding from the uncomfortable feelings of grief does not make them go away, and that if we don't face them now, when they are raw, they will be all the harder to handle later. The group becomes a safe place to expose our vulnerability, to grapple with our grief, and to help each other make it to the other side.

The planet continues to spin in its orbit, and winter eventually gives way to spring. Trees burst forth from dormancy with bright green leaves that shimmer and dance through summer. As the months unfold, the women in my grief support group bear witness as each of us navigates the rocky wilderness of bereavement at our own pace. Some have found the strength to move on, and others who are newer to the journey have taken their places.

By the time the leaves are, once again, performing their last fiery dance before they fall back to earth, almost a year of Mondays has passed. Almost a year of consciously confronting my grief. Somehow, I have survived my first year of being a motherless daughter.

Finally, the ache in my soul has begun to ease. But, by now, I also understand that the pain of losing my mother will never totally go away. It is, like Rachel described, "as if an elephant has taken up permanent residence in your living room. At first, it seems to take up all of the space and you can't bear the weight of its presence. Slowly, however, you realize it isn't going to leave, so you gradually adjust to its new place in your life. Sometimes, you even forget it is there. If not peace, you at least make friends with it."

I now see that joy and suffering are inextricably linked; one would not exist without the other. I have grieved deeply because I have loved deeply. Allowing myself to experience the raw pain over my mother's death has also enabled me to remember and relive the pure joy of sharing my life with her. In time, I have come to recognize the beauty inside the pain—that, had I not loved her so much, it would not have hurt so much to lose her. Now, if someone I know suffers a loss, I know that the best thing to say is simply, "I'm sorry. I am here for you." And to mean it.

Slowly, I am putting the weight back on that I lost during my mother's illness and also toning my muscles with weight training and yoga. I feel more alive than ever, and I have a renewed sense of interest in the world around me.

I look forward to daily walks with my black Lab, a surprise gift from a friend during my mother's last days. Together, we trace my mother's steps past the madroña trees that line the bluff and look across the ever changing waters of Puget Sound to the rugged Olympic mountains—her favorite view. I work part-time with children now, an intentional choice to remind myself that there is still innocence in this world. I am drawing and painting with a depth unknown before. And I am smiling again—not a forced smile, not the facade of a smile, but the real thing, a smile that is spontaneous and springs from true joy and carries laughter behind it.

It is another Monday. An old friend from high school has left a message on my answering machine suggesting an impromptu catch-up dinner. It's been several years since we've seen one another. I think of my plans to attend my grief group meeting that night and feel torn about what to do. I still have moments of despair; I am not ready to let go of the support that I am so grateful to have found. I want to be there for the others, as well. "Well, maybe this once," I hear myself say out loud.

I call my friend back and tell her I'll meet her at the restaurant. I know my other friends in the group will understand. After all, it is where they all hope to be one day . . . each in her own time.

—*Laurie McConnachie*

Some names in this story have been changed to protect the privacy of those individuals and their loved ones.

See What You Need

I was getting better, stronger. Not in a linear fashion of progression, where today is better than the last, but in a roller-coaster style—like, some days were great and others felt more like the bottom was dropping out of my stomach.

Occasionally, I went out with friends and transformed back into "Greeny," my fun alter-ego. But once your dad dies, you're never really the same. I wallowed (silently) in self pity and feelings of abandonment. Plus, my dad died of lung cancer midway through my freshman year of college, so I blamed him for doing it to himself, even though he had given up smoking nineteen years prior to his diagnosis. But when you're stuck at college, five hundred miles from home, and you're relatively new there, you do your best to plaster a phony grin on your face and pretend you are just as interested in the latest hook-up at the frat party as anyone else. It's hard for mopey kids to make friends, so I tried to keep everything as normal as possible, while inside, I vacillated between raging at the idiot smokers in my dorm building and crying during commercials depicting dads walking their daughters down the aisle.

Those I did let in saw only a portion of my pain. Many tried valiantly to think of something to say, but it felt awkward and forced for all of us. It's funny how, when you go to school far from home, you can forget to call your parents, forget to write them, forget your household rules and all the things they taught you. But when you're parent dies, you can't forget that. And, although I tried, for the sake of my own normalcy, my quest for the "normal" freshman year was impossible. I had faced something most of my peers wouldn't until middle age, and it had aged me twenty years. Still, I wasn't ready to look at it philosophically; I just wanted not to be that kid everyone sighs when they see.

Even the dean of students got involved. The day he summoned me to his office, all I could think about was that my lousy grades were going to get me kicked out. Then, my mom would be mad and my dad would be disappointed (from the great beyond), and I'd be that kid who couldn't make it through college.

"I've been speaking with your advisor," he began from deep in his chair. He looked at me with scrutinizing eyes.

I wondered if he was waiting for me to say something. But the lump in my throat choked any possibility of words. I nodded instead.

"She says you haven't come to see her and that she didn't even know of your father's passing."

I nodded again. This time he waited. I looked at the diplomas hanging on his wall from a small school I had never heard of. I wondered if you had to be top of your class to get a job like dean of students. What did he do other than expel people? If you had a serious problem, he would refer you to a therapist. So what did he really do?

He seemed to be allowing me to sort through all this in my head, because he did not change the subject or go on. He continued to look at me as he leaned forward.

Oh, God. Here it comes. He's going to toss me out. I'd felt relatively safe until he leaned forward. Everyone knows you can't expel someone from the depth of the chair, you have to get up close and personal, out of sympathy or aggression.

He apparently grew bored of my silence and proceeded anyway. "After looking over your transcript, it seems . . . "

I think he was talking at that point, but all I could hear was the thumping of my heartbeat in my ears. The heat of my own cheeks distracted me from trying to figure out where the school was that he graduated from, and the gurgling in my stomach brought to mind the sour face my mother would make when I returned to her doorstep.

"Did you hear me?"

I shook my head. Maybe if I didn't hear that he wanted to kick me out, maybe he wouldn't be able to repeat it. Maybe he'd feel sorry for me. I tried to imagine what my dad would do.

"You're a class short, and unless you want to fall behind and make it up in the summer, I thought I'd bring it to your attention. Of course, I understand if you'd like to take a lighter load this semester, but we pride ourselves on attention to students, and I didn't want you to fall through the cracks if the lighter course load had just been an oversight."

I shook my head and tried to make sense of what he had just said. I stopped just short of saying, "You're not kicking me out?" But then, I figured, why bring it to his attention?

So, together, we looked over which courses were still open. I chose medical ethics as a tribute to my father, who had spent nearly fifty years in the medical profession. (That, and I figured it would be easy.)

As it turned out, the open-ended debates over controversial medical subjects, such as abortion and the right to die, that I had expected were limited, and the class spent most of its time watching videos. I spoke little and offered my opinions even less. But I was right: the class was easy; after all, anyone can watch a video monitor. So we trudged through a semester of exciting topics, presented in the most mundane of ways, and all of us who had been hoping for lively discussion had tuned out by week two.

With a month left to go, we started a segment on reproductive rights featuring yet another video series. By this time, I was looking forward to the class's video format, because I used the time to catch up on my rest. The reproductive rights series didn't hold any more interest than the last series of videos. It focused on a panel of white, male doctors sitting around speaking, not even debating. We didn't even get any good arguments among them. Occasionally, the camera man (who must have been as bored as we were) panned the audience. There, sitting in the third row from the front, was my father, wearing the tan wool blazer that was his uniform.

A sick feeling pooled in the pit of my stomach, and I rubbed anxiously at my eyes. I was cracking up. I had heard about folks who saw dead people, and I didn't think things ended well for them. First,

I'd be thrown out of college for my less-than-stellar academic performance, then I was going to end up in the nut house. How proud my parents would be and how valuable they would think my over-priced tuition had been. But no matter how many times I opened and closed my eyes, Dad was still there watching the panel very intently.

I floated back to my dorm room on a cloud of dismay. My roommate, who barely noticed me on most days, told me to sit down because I looked like I was going to pass out. I went to bed for my usual afternoon nap but didn't sleep. I was restless, trying to decide if I should tell someone that I was seeing dead people—and not just any dead person, but my dad. Maybe I could make the dean of students' day and give him something juicy to deal with. Maybe he would just lock me up. Crazy people didn't fit in on this otherwise beautiful campus.

At dinner that night, I told my best friend, Jenny. "I think I saw my dad today."

"Really?" was all she could muster.

"Yeah. On a video. In class."

"You think it was really him? Maybe it was just a guy that looked like him."

I shook her off. His hair was like my dad's. He dressed like my dad (which was not exactly a compliment). He was the same age as my dad. What were the odds of two men at a medical ethics conference being identical?

As if she could read my mind, Jenny said, "A lot of people look alike. Or maybe you just dreamt it. You know how you're always 'resting' in class."

"Nah, it was him."

She nodded and smiled. I could already tell by the look in her eyes that she felt sorry for me. Sure, she had felt initial pity for me when my dad died, but the look she gave me now was different. It was the same look we gave the party-guy down the hall when he got kicked out of school the second week for selling drugs. She looked at me like she didn't think I was going to make it to graduation. I didn't blame her. I was questioning my abilities too.

For four straight weeks, I saw him. I watched him stretch, take notes, clear his throat, shift positions, and just be human again. By the end of the month, I was looking forward to my weekly "lunch date" with Dad. I got to see my dad in a professional setting, to see him in a way I wouldn't otherwise have been able to do. He was there nonfailingly, and I drew great comfort from seeing him.

The last week of my class, I felt like I would be saying goodbye to him forever, but I was somehow able to handle that. I was ready. It was like when you are starting your freshman year and you're filled with a potent mix of trepidation and exhilaration. You can't ever imagine wanting to say goodbye to the high school experience, but by the time the end comes, you're okay to leave, like what you've learned has made you more able to cope with what looms before you.

I can't say that the class added to my knowledge on medical ethics, but it gave me something that no one else could: It allowed me to spend eight more hours with my dad. The price of that was worth every penny of tuition.

At the end of the last class, I went up to the professor and told her my dad was on that video. She looked at me with sympathy (because when you attend a small college, everyone knows whose parents died midway through freshman year. I think they keep a list of those most likely to fail or crack up.).

"Would you like me to make a copy of it for you?"

I thought about it and then shook my head no. As much as I had enjoyed my time with him, I was worried that, upon playing it back (and pausing it, because you know I would have), I would see that the distinguished, gray-haired man I had been so convinced was my dad would turn out to be some stranger who looked nothing like him. It was time to get off the roller-coaster of grief and begin my steady healing process. As I looked into my professor's questioning eyes, I knew my dad was always going to be there, in every crowd I saw, out of the corner of my eye. He would always be there because he was in my heart and on my mind, and I didn't need a video to stay close to him. He would always be a part of me. And, ultimately, I would rather be satisfied with our last time spent together than to realize it had all been in my head.

—*Christina Smith*

To Infinity and Beyond

The verbal sparring started as one of those endearing brotherly games of one-upsmanship.

Nine-year-old to seven-year-old: "Okay, name the highest number you know."

"One-hundred-thousand-million-billion."

"I can name one higher than that: infinity!"

"Oh, yeah? Well, what about infinity plus one?"

"Infinity *plus* infinity."

"Infinity *times* infinity!"

The conversation drifted over to me, their somewhat overwhelmed mother, trying to pit her pin-sized smallness against the vastness of the visible world and the even greater vastness of the world of faith. Real Life Philosophy 101 had its moment, maybe a good five minutes, while I mulled life everlasting, considered infinity, and rinsed soapy dishes in the

sink. *How vast is infinity? How big is the biggest thing
you can imagine? How endless? How everlasting?*

Then, pondering infinity lost out to the immediate need of finding soccer balls for the night's
practice.

It was September, the start of school and a season
of colossal family holidays. My mother was the oldest
in her family. She and her middle sister shared a birthday, ten years apart, over Labor Day weekend. My
Aunt Mandy would be fifty-six, and for the first time
in her life, she would have a surprise birthday party.
All sorts of surreptitious arrangements were made,
including the stow-away of her daughter and new son-
in-law, who were flying from Chicago to Pittsburgh.
My mother and Mandy's younger brother, Joe, and
twin sister, Judy, would be part of the cross-country
rendezvous, too. Joe flew from his home in San Diego
to meet Judy in Arlington, Virginia. They dawdled on
their drive up to Pittsburgh, but still arrived early, so
cut a fairly wide swath around Mandy's house, miracu-
lously appearing on cue for the party.

The party was flawless. The surprise was genuine,
the guests were happy, the balloons were cheerful,
and the caterer was wonderful. People enjoyed each
other and the occasion for celebration—a tradition-
ally non–landmark birthday marked with the bash
of a lifetime. The day after, the far-flung brother and

his three sisters had a chance to loll by the pool and bask in each other's company. My sons and I laid claim to some of this time, which gave a real-life personality to the great-uncle they'd previously known only through pictures. Uncle Joe allowed the boys to splash him in the pool and then played get-back with big splashes and ferocious sounds. He remembered their favorite foods at lunchtime. He showed them how to make the signals that would make our doggy friend do tricks. He gave them each wooden boxes with special compartments to hold the quirky treasures that little boys keep.

The next day, he returned to Arlington for an extended visit with Judy.

A week later, my husband called me at work. He couldn't talk on the phone. "Meet me," he said.

As I drove, I whispered a prayer. I knew one of us was gone. I just didn't know who.

I turned numb when he said Joe had died that morning. Joe, fifty-three, was the king of practical jokers. For his older sister's surprise party, old-hippie Joe had cut his hair, shaved his moustache, and looked like the clean-cut heartbreaker posing in his high school graduation picture. His parting shot at our visit was to push me into the pool, glasses and all.

"I'll get you back," I promised. I never had the chance.

Joe died at his twin's house in Arlington.

Information came in dribbles. Eventually, we pieced together that he'd had his morning coffee on Judy's deck, gone upstairs to the bathroom, and never came back down. The paramedics tried their best. Joe left behind corneas that would help someone see and three sisters with hearts slashed wide open.

The four siblings had been in their twenties and thirties when they buried their mother, a victim of a heart attack—apparently, the same thing that took Joe. For more than ten years after their mother's death, the family watched their once vibrant father turn into a lonely, sickly man, isolated by emphysema that left him gasping for breath even as he crossed the room. He had died just four years before his only son.

The family had worked through other problems and ailments, including a newborn who had suffered but survived a stroke. But no trials aged these sisters like Joe's death.

Mandy and Mom caught the next flight from Pittsburgh to Arlington.

Two days later, I picked up two drawn, middle-aged strangers at the airport. The ride home was painfully quiet. Mom sat in the back seat of the van. The usual domain of her frisky grandsons was shrouded in silence. Mandy rode in the passenger seat, clutching a tissue and silently watching the guardrails pass. In her lap, she cradled what looked like an oversized cigar box. I learned later she held Joe's remains.

I drove us to my house for dinner. They shuffled around on their plates what was supposed to be comfort food, eating almost nothing, and then asked to go home.

Getting back in the car, Mandy nearly sat on the box. "Oh, Joe, I'm sorry!" she said. She flashed a mischievous smile. "He'd think that's funny." Then her eyes welled up.

Until the moment he left us, Joe had been very alive. There was no sickness, no premonition, no warning. The family, especially my mother and her sisters, took it very hard. As for me, I had small boys to attend to, but as wonderful diversions as they were, I'd find myself crying while I folded laundry or in the pre-dawn darkness.

The rest of the world continued on, though. At that time, our country was preparing to send John Glenn back into space for a second time. It's amazing, I told the boys, because the trip is so rigorous and John Glenn is old for an astronaut, older than their Grandpap.

Seven-year-old Christopher tried to absorb the thought of someone that old making such a remarkable journey. He peppered me with questions. "How far is the trip?" "How many moons will he pass?" "What else will he see?" I answered each question to the best of my ability.

Then Christopher's baby blue eyes latched onto mine. "Is John Glenn older than Uncle Joe?"

"Of course," I said. "John Glenn is seventy-seven. Uncle Joe was fifty-three."

"No, Mom. Uncle Joe is dead, so Uncle Joe is infinity."

Christopher's clarity stopped me in my tracks. Joe is now infinity. He is without end. He is seamless, boundless, everlasting. He is as endless as an azure summer sky over the soccer field, beyond the horizon over the ocean, wider than this galaxy or the next. Joe is infinity times infinity, the biggest number anyone could ever conceive.

Then, just as suddenly as he'd spouted those words of wisdom, Christopher ran outside to play, unaware of the priceless lesson about "life ever after, amen" that he had just unknowingly taught his own mother. But each time I look into the heavens, I remember it. This lesson—that Joe will be part of us forever—will stay with me always. For infinity.

—*Karen Ferrick-Roman*

Don't Be Brave

"You're a wise woman; what are God's words for me today?"

I was dumbstruck. *How could Lois ask me that? I wondered.*

Time seemed to stand still as I looked into my dear friend's eyes, red and puffy from a week of tears and lack of rest. I glanced quickly around the small hospital room. My husband was quietly conversing with Rob, Lois's husband. Their seven-year-old son, James, lay near death in the unkempt bed. He was moaning softly. The scabbed marks on his wrists and ankles betrayed the use of restraints that had tied him down during his earlier seizures. Rob had since convinced the hospital staff that the restraints were not needed if he lay on the bed with his feverish son. He stroked James's face and arms with a damp cloth and murmured memories and endearments in an effort to keep him cool and calm. James was not only having complications from malaria and asthma, he was also experiencing heart problems caused by the differing medicines. The next morning, James would be flown on a life flight to Paris, France, from the small West African country where we all served as missionaries.

I closed my eyes and prayed. *Lord, you said you would put words in our mouths. I don't know what to say here.*

When I opened my eyes, the movement of time was restored. Lois looked expectantly at me. I opened my mouth and only four words came out: "Lois, don't be brave." These were not words that my psychology professor would have approved, nor were they words that came from my experience as a pastor's wife or missionary. In fact, I could not believe they had left my mouth at all, and my hand flew to cover my mouth as if to shove the unwanted words back.

Lois and I stared at each other with eyes popped as wide as they could be. We both knew that if these were, indeed, the words of God, then James was going to die. Neither one of us wanted to acknowledge that, so we said nothing.

My husband finished his time with Rob by saying a prayer. Lois and I hugged a wordless goodbye. The next day, James died in Paris.

Their family was called back to the United States for a time to regroup. Lois and Rob had to decide whether to continue in their present missionary assignment or choose another vocation. Their younger children, one of whom had nearly died on the same bed as his brother, had to regain their health.

While the family healed and considered their future, the close-knit ex-patriot community made up of many nationalities and occupations all waited for news. It came in dribs and drabs from mutual friends who bumped into Lois and Rob while on home assignment.

Several months after James passed away, Christine, a mutual friend said, "Amy, I just saw Lois in the states, and she gave me a message for you." She tilted her head and seemed to wonder if she had gotten the message correctly. "She told me that you would understand; she said, 'Tell Amy that I'm not being brave.' Does that make sense?"

I nodded that it did, indeed, make sense.

I was in misery. I pictured Lois as I had last seen her, with red, puffy eyes and a broken heart. What had I done?

A year after James's death, his parents and younger siblings returned as missionaries to the same region in West Africa. We were happy to have them back and amazed at their resiliency through the past year.

A few weeks after the family's arrival, Lois decided to hold a memorial time in which all their friends could say a few words about James as a closing to the formal grieving time. The ex-patriot community formed a large circle in the family's living room. Almost everyone shared their recollections of James. He had been a very active and likeable kid, so tales abounded. Lois and Rob nodded at some memories and shook their heads at others. Some of the stories were new to them. I said nothing.

After everyone was finished, Lois noticed my silence and spoke up. "There is someone here who has not spoken yet. I want to thank her. A year ago, when James was in the hospital, she told me, 'Lois, don't be brave.' If ever words came directly from the mouth of God, it was then. I didn't want to hear those words at that moment, but wisdom came with time.

"You see," Lois continued, "I was raised a military brat. I knew how I was to act at all times. Soldiers don't cry. Soldiers don't let others know when they are hurting. Soldiers face every situation with self-control. Soldiers are brave. In my life, up to that point, I had always acted like a soldier. Yet, over the past year, with a loss so great, I could not do that. I was broken in two by James's death.

"But with Amy's words, God had given me permission to cry on the shoulders of strangers. He had given me authorization to tell grocery clerks and store managers why I was weeping as I bought only two sets of school supplies. God allowed me to scream and sob uncontrollably if I needed to. I didn't need to be brave, and I wasn't. By revealing my brokenness, I have managed to make it through this year. I have discovered God in the unlikeliest of people and places. People have listened by the hour as I remembered my funny bundle of joy that was taken away. I know now that I don't need to be brave. God has touched my heart. I'm not God's soldier; I'm His beloved daughter, and He grieves with me."

As Lois spoke, I asked God's forgiveness for not trusting that he knew her better than I did and certainly better than my psychology professor did. Then I returned Lois's smile. There were miles left to travel on her road of grief, but with God's grace and with the loving support of others, Lois could walk its entire length on her own two feet and at her own pace, trusting she'd find comfort when she couldn't be brave.

—*Amy Crofford*

My Father Heard Music

It's fair to say that much of my father's day was spent thinking about, listening to, or playing the music that shaped his identity and wove itself around his everyday existence. Bill Healey was an early riser who belted out one of several songs each morning to wake his six sleeping children. His office was an elementary school, his desk, a piano.

When my oldest brother was in the second grade, his teacher asked the children, one by one, to name where their fathers worked. When she looked at my brother, awaiting his answer, he hid his head in his hands and cried in shame. The teacher pulled him aside, thinking the worst.

"What is it, Billy?" she asked.

"My father doesn't have a job. He still goes to school," he whispered.

Later that day, my mother told him his dad was a music teacher. He couldn't wait to tell the class.

"Bill, what do you want for dinner?" my mother would call from the kitchen, her fingers wrapped around the Manhattan my father had just concocted, the red cherry bobbing in the golden liquid.

His booming voice would sing, "Food, glorious food—hot sausage and mustard!"

"*Really*, Bill!" she'd say, smiling to herself.

Eyes twinkling, he would wink at me and continue belting out the song from the other room, "While we're in the mood, cold jelly and custard!"

Mom put together dinner for nine every night, complete with mashed potatoes, gravy, and always the right accompaniment for the meat, as required by Dad: cranberries for turkey, mint jelly for lamb, and applesauce for pork. But we had meatloaf most often.

Grandma lived with us in the "apartment" downstairs, which was really a renovated garage. We felt like we lived in a palace, even though it was just one of many houses in Long Island, New York.

Dad presided over his home like the king in the *King and I*. Sitting in his high-back chair by the big front window, clad in his starched, white button-down shirt and dress pants after school, he rested his cocktail on the hand-me-down marble-top table and smacked his lips. The room filled up with kids, some running in and out to play, some staying to listen to the mysterious adult talk that always took place just before dinner. There were often stray kids in our house. The neighborhood was teeming with children of all ages, and ours was the one house everyone wanted to be in. It was the fun house.

At 6:00, Dad would call out the front door, "Billy, John. Dinner!" Then marching back to the table he'd sing to himself, "You say potat-o and I say pa-tah-to." Like a character meandering through a musical, he would burst out into song several times a day.

On the night his own father died, Dad went straight to the piano and said in a sad voice, "This is dedicated to Pop."

He played a piano piece called, "Oh Breathe Not His Name," written by the Irish poet Thomas Moore. His shoulders, arms, and fingers leaned into the piano as he looked upward, eyes closed, and played as though deep in prayer. His personal and complicated emotions were poured into his beloved instrument.

Mom pulled us aside and whispered us a story that became part of our family folklore. "Your father played the piano all night for his mother when she was dying. He had been called home from the Air Force to see her one last time. She was his first piano teacher, and his music was the last sound she heard on Earth."

As children, we were somewhat shocked that our father could have such a solemn side.

On most ordinary days, Dad was all about show tunes and Sinatra or Joplin, jump and jive, and he played carols at the annual Christmas party, which grew to be a major holiday event made elegant by his festive style and dramatic flourishes punctuating the end of each song. Over the years, Dad played in a band at weddings and events to earn extra cash. On Sundays, he played the church organ at St. Anthony's of Padua, which meant we got to sit in the balcony when we wanted, as long as we sang with the choir and didn't try to balance our hymnals on the railing that towered over the pews.

Dad was the maestro of every party, and he loved to throw parties.

"You're sixteen, you're beautiful, and you're mine!" He'd sing the only few words he knew over and over each time he saw me walk by at my sweet-sixteen party.

That evening, he attempted two of my contemporary signature songs on keyboard—"Love Grows Where My Rosemary Goes" and Neil Diamond's "Cracklin' Rosie"—with my brother on drums, my other brother on sax, and a few friends playing guitar. My friends and I snuck beers and had a wild time dancing and secretly meeting in the dark corners of the playroom.

"Quiet in the balcony!" Dad would yell when he heard smooching.

In retirement, Dad was the accompanist for several community theatre productions and went through a musical love affair with Linda Ronstadt when she released her album, "What's New," in 1983 with all the oldies produced in a sultry style. He'd walk around his yard singing, "I've got a crush on you, sweetie-pie." He also developed a thing for Bette Midler. "She's got spunk!" he would say.

When I gave birth to twin daughters, Dad sang to them and bounced them on his knees: "Ride a cock horse to Banbury Cross / To see a fine lady upon a white horse / With rings on her fingers and bells on her toes / She shall have music wherever she goes."

Years later, he taught the girls to waltz on my kitchen floor. My daughter Mary wrote her college entrance essay about the transformational moment when her grandfather had plunked her down next to him on his piano bench at age six and serenaded her with "You Must Have Been a Beautiful Baby." She is a musical theater major now.

My father remained good-natured, gregarious, and musical to the end. He spent the final two years of his life at an assisted-living facility, where he played piano daily for anyone who would assemble to listen. He often played the same tune over and over, not remembering he had played it moments before. And, though he could not recall the year, the day, or even what season it was outside, he could remember us and the notes to any song, and he could play without sheet music.

The night before he passed away, he could not get out of bed. He had been moved from the hospital to his room at Morningside, and my mother and I had just put in an anxious twelve-hour day worried about him. After dinner, I went back to see him one more time. He was in obvious pain. I called him "Gandhi," because he was thin and frail and possessed an otherworldly quality. It was springtime, but he felt chilly, so I tucked his sheet in tight and added a white cotton blanket, pulling it up under his bare bony arms—the arms that were always moving.

"What song am I playing, Rosie?" he croaked. His eyelids fluttered and a smile played on his dry lips. His fingers, like brittle twigs, played the invisible ivory keys across the top of his own sunken abdomen.

"I don't know, Dad," I said.

"We used to sing it in the car, you and me." He emphasized each note with dancing fingers across the cotton blanket.

"Moon River?"

His smile grew wider. To keep from crying, I sang a few lines and remembered us dancing at my wedding thirty years ago as the band played this song. I closed my eyes and felt his strong arms leading me in sweeps across the floor beneath the tent in his backyard.

"We're after the same rainbow's end . . . "

My father died later that night, no doubt hearing a symphony in his own musical mind.

He left us with a lifetime of beautiful memories to comfort us in his absence. I need only hear one of a thousand songs he played and sang for me, and Dad is right there by my side again.

—*Rosemary Rawlins*

Aunt Nancee Danced

On Thursday, at the Greenwood Park Shopping Mall, I danced on the sidewalk outside of Lazarus department store. Some might find it odd that I, a grown woman, would "Shuffle Off to Buffalo" in front of a busy mall. But if you knew my little niece Erin, you would understand.

Erin isn't really "little" anymore. A junior at Purdue University, she stands over six feet tall. To me, though, she is and always will be my precious little niece.

Dugger is a small town. A tight-knit community where you know the neighbor next door and his family, even the names of his animals; where, if you step out of line, another parent will telephone your home and inform your family. More than one Dugger parent had called my mother when they saw me ride my bicycle in the street. Years later, other Dugger parents would call Erin's mother when they saw Erin riding her four-wheeler too fast. Some things never change. . . .

Erin and I both graduated from Dugger-Union High School. Although I'm more than a few years older than Erin, we had several of the same high school teachers.

I watched with amazement as Erin sailed through her high school years. When she would talk about that boring government teacher, I would laugh. True, it was difficult to stay awake in his class; I know because I'd been in it. I sometimes wondered whether Erin and I sat in the same row or perhaps even the same chair that I had all those years ago.

When Erin spiked the ball for the volleyball team, I held my breath and then cheered her athletic prowess. I was there to take pictures when she was named Basketball Homecoming Queen. But when the time came and they announced her name, I couldn't move. My husband had to take all the photographs that night. When she received her diploma, I could not contain my tears any more than I could contain my pride as I listened to her valedictorian speech.

Erin has grown into a lovely young woman with a zest for life. With her yellow hair flowing down around her shoulders, sparkling violet eyes, refined facial features, and slender, well-proportioned figure, she is special to look at, a real head-turner. Plus, her personality absolutely shines! She can be as gregarious as a Mardi Gras carnival and as lighthearted as a soap bubble. Yet, she has the ability to focus and the gumption to reach for her dreams.

Her good grades have continued at Purdue, where she is also a member of the drill team. Erin has that rare combination of beauty, intelligence, motivation, and enthusiasm that might make her sorority sisters envious. Beyond that, my niece is a good kid. And she is my friend.

Erin came home for spring break this week. Many of her friends went to Florida, the usual spring vacation locale, but Erin opted to stay in Indiana with her family and her boyfriend. And she wanted to go shopping with her Aunt Nancee. So, on Thursday, we met up at Greenwood Park Shopping Mall to do as they advertise: "Shop like you mean it."

Erin bought clothes at Paul Harris, and we giggled as she bought intimate apparel at Ayres department store. We stuffed our tummies at the food court and found new purple tennis shoes for Erin at the Shoe Rack. In the novelty store Spencer Gifts, she pointed out what I could buy and send her at Purdue: "The Crazy Limber Louie Jr.," a big, yellow feathered bird that bounces up and down. She wanted to hang it in the sorority house. I took note of where it was located in the store.

We stopped and tossed a penny in the water fountain near the Camera Shop. We each made a wish. I can't remember what I wished for, but I remember I had to borrow a penny from her.

As we shopped, we talked. I teased her about her cat, Hank. Somehow, Hank always knows when Erin pulls her car into the driveway.

We are both hooked on the McDonald's Monopoly game. The odds of winning are based on one particular piece. Erin knew which game pieces she needed, and I promised to send her the game pieces if and when I found them.

Having spent more than enough money and loaded down with big bags, we decided to call it a day. Her boyfriend was waiting at home, and she was excited. I walked her to her car, which was parked in front of Lazarus department store, on the opposite side of the mall from where my car was parked.

"I love you, Aunty Nancee" she said, giving me a hug. I could smell Red Door, her favorite fragrance, in her hair.

"I love you too, Erin," I said. "I'll dance as you drive away."

"Okay," she said with a grin.

I watched, smiling, as she unlocked the car, tossing her hair from her face. I glanced at my watch; it was exactly 6:00 P.M. I had other things to do.

No, not so, I thought. Take time to smell the roses. Yeah, I'll do it. I will dance for Erin.

It was a silly thing to do, I guess, for a forty-year-old lady. If anyone saw me, they might have taken me for a daffy blonde. But who cares? On Thursday, outside the glass outer doors of Lazarus department store, I danced on the sidewalk—"Shuffle off to Buffalo," the only vaudeville step I know—as my niece Erin drove off.

Her car stopped at the stop sign, and when she saw me there, dancing, she laughed. I thought I saw a flash of light in her eyes as she waved goodbye.

On the way home, Erin used her cell phone to call her dad, saying she had spent most of his money and she should be home soon.

Erin never made it home from the Greenwood Park Shopping Mall. Less than fifteen minutes after talking to her dad, another automobile hit her car broadside. Even with her seat belt on, the side impact was too much for her. Despite the efforts of the rescue units, my niece's life was over. She was only twenty.

I wonder if five more minutes of shopping would have made a difference. I wish we had tried on one more pair of shoes. Or walked to the pet store just to look, like she'd suggested.

I cry. I question why. Why Erin? Her hopes and dreams and happiness were not supposed to end. Friends listen, but they seem at a loss for words. There are no words. They try to understand, to console me. But how can they? They did not know my niece, did not know how special she was.

But I knew Erin, and I loved her. So, on Thursday, at Greenwood Park Shopping Mall, outside Lazarus department store, I danced on the sidewalk, to make her laugh. And it is that image of Erin's radiant smile and sparkling eyes—along with the memories of our wonderful last day together and of everything that made my niece the special person she was—that I try to hold on to as I face the days and years ahead, unfathomably, without her.

—*Nancee Harrison*

Hit

Orelia and I were riding home on the bus. I had only just come back to school. I was showing her some scrunchies I'd made in home-ec class when she asked, "So, do you miss your mom?"

I nodded.

"Do you want to cry?"

I shook my head.

She waited. "It's okay if you want to cry."

"I know," I said. We *were* sitting in the back of the bus; no one would see.

She squinted. Finally, she said with authority: "It just hasn't hit you yet."

I nodded, but I really didn't think so.

The days that followed the accident were odd ones. I was the oldest of four kids born in quick succession, almost too much for two working parents.

We were used to running a little wild; our parents macro-managed. We definitely weren't accustomed to the kind of glaring attention that became focused on each of us when our mother was in the hospital. Aunts came to help, and neighbors and churchy types—all of them with their high hopes, homemade goodies, and different sets of rules. It was bewildering.

The special treatment extended to the hospital, too. There was no such thing as visiting hours for us. The nurses offered to take us to see *Aladdin* in the theater. I was allowed to spend as much time lost inside myself as I wanted. I frequented the chapel.

After my mom died, the oddness continued. I was invited to sit at the popular table in the lunchroom. I was sent to see the school counselor. I could turn in my homework late.

At my brother's school, they even set up a memorial garden for her, because my mom had been helping someone when she died. There had been an accident just outside her church as everyone was leaving. I wasn't there, but I could imagine hearing her say, "Hello? Is everyone all right? I'm a nurse." She would have used her calm voice, the one she used whenever there might be trouble.

It was icy. A lot of cars lost control that night. But it was a big truck that hit my mom as she stood at the side of the road, helping a driver from a previous accident.

I don't remember the funeral at all. Supposedly, we sat in the front pew—all four of us numb-with-shock kids and our grief-stricken dad. Supposedly, a lot of people attended the memorial service.

I do remember walking up to the church; someone mentioned how big it was. My dad said that, when they built the addition, they got ripped off by a smooth-talking contractor and their own too-trusting ways. He never did like her church.

Later that same year, a rally was held at school. The program was about the pain of losing someone who has been killed in a drunk-driving accident. People kept looking at me. It was the perfect time to cry. I tried, but I couldn't lose myself in the emotion.

Five years later, I did cry at school, but by then, it was a different experience. I was in swing choir, wearing my silver sequin vest and the black satin gloves that came up past my elbows. Normally, such suggestiveness was frowned upon, but this was for the choir.

We were rehearsing for a Mother's Day concert. It was early in the morning and the energy was low. To perk everyone up, the director asked each of us to say one thing we appreciated about our moms.

There were touching stories everywhere. I was nearly panicked, but when the director's face met mine she said, "Oh, I'm so sorry."

She had gone to school with my mother, so she knew.

I cried.

One day, I met a man. He was a charming-enough suitor, but when he suggested we visit my mom's gravesite, I didn't want to. He even offered to supply flowers, but I begged off.

I thought that simply wasn't part of my life anymore.

At the time, my sister had been hanging out with my brother a lot. She called to say that he often talked about Mom when he got drunk.

It was strange, because we really didn't talk about Mom.

"He gets all upset and he cries, and he says how much he misses her," she said.

He was *crying* about Mom? True, he had always been special to her, almost like a favorite, but it had been years. To still be that emotional when he was talking about Mom? How odd.

When I got married, I didn't think to miss my mom at the bridal shower, the wedding, or the reception. As a newlywed, I didn't wonder how she'd made the transition or long to call her when my new husband and I had a lover's quarrel.

But when I got pregnant, I had so many questions: How much weight had she gained in her first trimester? Her second? Her third? How long until she lost it all afterward—because she did lose it all, right? Most of all, I really wanted to ask, Just how much was my life going to change, anyway?

My dad was excited about the pregnancy, but he is not the kind of person whom you ask these questions.

What made it even worse was that my mom had been a visiting nurse. And her specialty had been counseling new mothers.

I had never missed her so much.

My therapist loves the movies. Her advice often comes couched in plot lines or with a recommendation for a film she feels has some therapeutic value. But she throws her hands in the air when she talks about how therapists are portrayed in the movies. "They're always nuts!" she laments.

It's not easy being a therapist, and it's not easy explaining you're in therapy, either, but my relationship with my therapist is special. People say the universe sends you exactly the people you need and, in my case, the universe sent my therapist.

She is a warm lady, full of good advice and motherly ways. I picked her nearly at random, and yet we are so well suited, it's hard to believe it was only chance.

Like my father, my therapist raised four children on her own, and she shares his religion. So, even as I rail against him and give my opinion of his multiple failings, she remains objective. She empathizes with us all.

She also understands my somewhat solitary, scholarly ways. She is one of the few people who has encouraged me to read and write *more*. She keeps piles of books in her office, alongside candles and a homemade throw, and over the years she has also kept a space for me where I can talk about my mother.

And so she knows that, like me, my mom loved to read poetry and keep journals.

My mother is not what I went into therapy to discuss, but she often comes out.

My therapist has been instrumental in helping me find my own way to grieve. As it turns out, my grieving has nothing to do with the five stages.

I love books, and I have found great comfort reading about how tragedy can echo through a family. I like Robert Hellenga's *The Fall of a Sparrow* and Alice Sebold's *The Lovely Bones*. They touch grief gracefully. They don't hurry it. They don't try to sanitize it or put it under wraps or make it heal. They give grief its due.

I always knew mourning was not something to cling to, but what took me longer to realize is it is also not something to overcome.

Grief fits into my life now. It has its place. My mother's invisible hands continue to touch the threads of my life, even through her absence, and I want them to. My life moves on in all its myriad ways, but my grief over the fact that she is gone is a reminder, a testament, and a tribute to our enduring bond.

—Kate Tapper

Putting Things Away

I put away my husband's things in fits and starts. His baseball caps. His hunting bow. Some bills from long ago. This pile for the memory. That pile for the trash. All haunted stories of love and journeys never to be taken again.

His Labrador dog, the color of high-end chocolate, weaves in and out, sniffing. She is lost in her last bird hunt with him, when she barked everything away, or at the beach, where she chased the sticks he threw. She whines and wags her tail in joyous measure. She remembers.

I, on the other hand, sit with these precious things: His stories from college in which he used our sons as characters. The essay about his dream garage. His maps from a geology trip. Arrowheads and crystals trapped in ore from eighteen hundred feet below the earth.

Exactly, what am I to do? Sudden widowhood at fifty-five was not on my horizon. But here I am, on my own.

The world is full of images of widowhood. The "merry widow." Scarlet O'Hara with her la-de-dah. Jackie Kennedy behind her veil. They mourn, or pretend to mourn, and show us the way. Others write books on grief and give advice—like *How to Widow*. But where is the guide for putting things away?

"Get rid of the clothes right away," some friends opined, even offering to help.

I could do that, but it doesn't come as easy as you think. Clothes have meaning and stories to tell. His running tees. His jogging togs. Is it strange that I often wear them to bed? His fleece jacket. His leather gloves. I make a pile for Goodwill. Another for my sons to try on. And some for me. I'm not ready yet.

I sold his drift boat, custom-made and used for barely a year. His wading boots. I put them all away into my pile of memories of forests and steelhead streams.

There are letters from Vietnam written to his parents when he was just nineteen years old. The first says, "Hey, Mom and Dad. Guess where I am at now? About 45 miles east of Ankhe, in the 5th Special Forces Camp. Two radio operators were needed . . . so they flew us in." The last sums it all: "You spend a year in the sewer system waiting for the water to back up. Then come and tell me how much fun you had." These letters make me cry.

The brown dog, with eyes the color of beer-bottle glass and boundless energy, brings me a ball to play with and licks my face. *Don't worry. Everything will be all right.* She knows. My husband worked as a geologist nearly two states away, coming home every ten days. A lonely life. He sought a buddy to greet him when he came back to his rental place after work. He had hunted with a dog when he was a boy. He had always wanted a chocolate Lab, but we hadn't had a dog in several years. I said I was willing. After finding an ad for pure-bred puppies in a Spokane newspaper, he drove a hundred miles to buy one.

It was a cold February day when the puppies' owner opened his garage door, releasing nineteen pups born to two different litters, to the snowy driveway. Black, straw, and chocolate, they were a vision of little tails and pudgy heavenly bodies swirling around one sun—my husband.

"I picked up one of the chocolates I liked," he told me later, "then put it down for another. I don't know if I ever got the same one back."

At least he accomplished his plan. The first night home with him, the eight-week-old pup slept in his makeshift bed on the floor.

I met the brown dog a week later. Sweet with puppy-tummy smell and as plump as a furry bon-bon, she burst into the house with explicit joy as she discovered the cats and socks lying on the floor. The first of my $37.95 bras was destroyed the next day. We were not off to a good start.

Over the months, she came home every ten days, growing from baby to rangy teenager. The household was never prepared. Cats scattered. I put things on high shelves and resigned myself to diminishing under-wear. My husband worried that I would never like her. But I did. She had a *joie de vivre* that couldn't be denied. But she was still my husband's dog. When he suddenly lost his job, they were both home for good.

Having the brown dog full-time was a new chal-lenge. For one, she chose my side of the bed. She pressed up against my legs, and when she dreamed, she kicked. I had no room to move. She was ordered down, but she always came back, her tongue panting with innocence.

Over time, she calmed down. Came when I called. Sat when I said, "Sit."

Before she came into our lives, whenever my hus-band was home, we walked together. A runner by nature, he took time away from his favorite passion to be with me. We explored the changing shape of our town, walking down to the harbor and back. When the brown dog arrived, a natural in water, we began to take walks on a local beach. Sometimes, the tide was in, crashing on the pebbly shore. Other times, it pulled far out, exposing hard pan mud flats that went on for over two miles. Tromping along in our boots, she ran ahead of us looking for sticks and the neighborhood collection of blue heron that spread out at the water's edge like swizzle sticks on a platter. When my husband came home for good, the walks became daily adventures that went on no matter the weather. Whether it froze or rained, we bundled up and went forth. For ten months. It was a blessed heaven, as we talked and watched or said nothing at all.

My husband died suddenly, alone. Did the brown dog stay with him? Sound an alarm? I'll never know. The very next day, she was up and ready for her walk. But over the days, weeks, and months that followed, she sometimes seemed confused and at a loss. If she saw any red car or truck, she bounced after them, seeking his face. She ran to any man she encountered. She was still his dog.

Once on the beach, a month after his death, I took the brown dog there to perform my daily ritual of hanging tough and grieving. A man approached me, and when she saw him, she sprinted toward him, her tail spinning. Frightened, the stranger recoiled, then yelled at me.

I burst into tears. "She wasn't coming to hurt you," I said. "She was coming to you with joy."

When I explained that the dog thought he was my dead husband, he put his head down. "Sorry. Sorry."

That was nearly seven years ago.

Today, my underthings are bite-free. The cat sleeps on the bed. The brown dog with the name of an espresso drink, Mocha, is mine. She runs ahead of me, leaping over logs in the path beneath cedar and fir trees. The little grove bursts with new leaf vigor. *Life goes on*, she says, and shows me how to do it. At night, she lays at my feet—my companion, my sweetest, dearest friend.

I'm not going to write about grief anymore. I am stronger. I have purpose and direction in my life. I have my sons to remind me of the one I lost. Our first grandchild, a beautiful baby girl, was born a few months ago.

But his dog, this final connection to the life we had together, of walking on beaches and fishing at streams . . . Some day, I will have to put away this silly, lovely, brown dog.

—*Janet Oakley*

A Wink and a Moo

After my mom died, I wanted nothing to do with her. That may sound strange. How could I have anything to do with her? She was dead!

You've got to understand. I come from a long line of people who talk to their dearly departed loved ones. Not only talk, but get answers, too.

After Grandma Flo died, my family whiffed her signature Lily of the Valley perfume in our house whenever she wanted to grab our attention. "What do you think Grandma is trying to tell us?" Dad would puzzle. Sometimes, she was more direct. "Art!" my dad heard her wavery voice call his name one afternoon. Moments later, the phone rang; her house had finally sold.

My mom was one of my best friends. So you'd think I would have welcomed her signs from the other side, her appearances in my dreams. But I snubbed her. My reaction made no sense to me.

We'd enjoyed our mother-daughtership, especially since the vacation we'd taken together seventeen years earlier. Our connection and our ongoing conversation had made that road trip from Chicago to Tampa feel like a grand adventure. All the static we'd endured during my adolescent years seemed to fly out the car window the moment Mom started mooing at the cows on the side of the road as we drove through the Illinois farmlands just south of the city. Suddenly, my mother was more than just my mom—she was a human being. A fun, playful, nonjudgmental, inquisitive, interesting, compassionate person. Moo-Mom.

More important, for thousands of miles, she sat side-by-side with me, supporting me, as I drove away from my perfectly loving first husband and into a new life with a new love, never once criticizing my choice.

I wish I could have been as accepting nearly twenty years later when she was rushed to the hospital at age eighty-three. My whole being felt chilled and tender with fear. She seemed oddly detached.

"I'm just floating," she'd say, waving one hand in the air. "Ta-ta. *Au revoir*," she'd call when we family members left for the night. "Love and light."

While Mom seemed distant, maybe even euphoric, when we left every night, my sisters and I would return to our parents' home feeling traumatized, each in our own way.

I felt powerless, frantic, and confused. How could she be leaving? And so nonchalantly? Not that I wished for one second of drama or pain. But I wanted to talk about it. We'd always been so open about everything. Years before, Mom had carefully selected the Psalms and hymns for her own funeral and filed them for safe keeping. Proud of her choices, she boasted about her plans, and every once in awhile, she casually reminded us of where they were filed. When she grew weary of travel, she simply said, "I'll see Europe after I die. That way I won't have to worry about what food I can eat or sitting on planes."

But when her health suddenly declined, she instantly seemed to disconnect from the family. It was as though she wanted to take what would become her last journey alone and had interest only in short pit stops with my sisters and me. The changes in her physical condition and in her attitude were so sudden and so unlike my Moo-Mom that it was disconcerting.

Six months before Mom's unexpected hospitalization and my mad race home to see her, perhaps, unbelievably, for the last time, I'd flown in from my home in Tucson for my twice yearly visit to my parents' home in Chicago. While sitting in the living room, writing, I was struck by the image of me looking up at a star someday in the distant future after my mom had died. I knew she was that star, looking down at me with love.

My completely healthy mother was in the middle of clipping newspaper articles when I told her about my vision. "Oh," she smiled up at me casually. "That's nice, Kitty Cat."

At the time, I did not take the clue that this might be my last "normal" visit with my mother. I was simply happy that we could share something that others might consider silly.

I longed for that kind of openness and intimacy now, for her to let me in and help answer all the questions swirling around in my mind. *What was happening to her? Did she know she was dying, even though no doctor would ever speak that word? How did her body and spirit really feel? Was she ready? Why now? Would she miss us? Why wouldn't she talk about it? Why couldn't I ask?*

It took all my energy just to be in her presence, and my heart shredded while she chatted about my sisters, nieces, and me forming a "butterfly club." With urgency, she had me take notes, as if I knew exactly what she was talking about.

"Good," she said after I'd written down "Butterfly Club" and then listed our names on the notepad she kept by her hospital bed. She had always been a passionate note-taker, and I knew this act soothed something inside her. For unknown reasons, our first club task was to get her multicolored scarves from her closet . . . and do what with them? I never found out.

Soon after, she could no longer speak. But she'd wink an eye and give us the okay sign with her fingers. Finally, three weeks later, as she lay immobile in her hospital bed, with her eyes closed, a tube stuck down her throat, and her hands restrained so she wouldn't pull out that tube, she erupted into a grin.

My sister Michele and I stared at each other. She held one of Mom's hands and I held the other.

"I love you, Moo-Mom," I said, crying. And I swear I felt a thump on my left shoulder. Not a tiny tap. A big wallop.

I looked behind me. There was Dad crumpled up on a chair near the window, being supported by our minister.

Mom? Was that her? Had she slipped out of her body and pushed me?

Nope. I—one of the universe's biggest believers in signs—didn't think so. It was just a coincidence. Or my imagination.

Mom died later that night.

For months afterward, I could feel her energy around me but would not turn to it. And I couldn't move on.

Friends suggested that I write her letters and drop them in a basket. Or concoct a new e-mail address and send my heart to her there. "Why don't you tie some yarn to tree branches in her honor?" said one of my editors. "Birds will take it and add it to their nests. It will become something new."

No. No. And no again. It was okay for John Edward to talk to spirits, but not me, not my mom. She slips out without so much as a howdy-do and now she wants to talk? Too painful. Sorry. Gotta go.

I carried on that way for quite some time. It wasn't until two years after she'd left the planet that I realized what might have been obvious to anyone else. Mom had been communicating with me—with my whole family—in every way she could. In and out of the hospital; in and out of her body. Through the language of butterflies, wallops on the shoulder, winks, and A-OK signs. The multicolored scarves? We fluttered them at her funeral service.

Who's to say what kind of language people in transition use to communicate with their loved ones? It's just like intuition. Intuition speaks to each of us in whatever way we can hear it: Through songs on the radio or images that flash in our minds. Someone says exactly the right thing at the right time. Answers to prayers make instant sense or they come in clues we have to decipher, just like in a scavenger hunt. One of my friends says that trying to listen to his inner voice is like playing an elaborate game of charades.

I knew all that. But how could I embrace it? I wanted Mom here, eating pretzels, wiping fudge from her face, laughing at old sit-coms.

Then, a few months ago, a box arrived in the mail. My sister Diane had warned me about it. "I've got a surprise for you! I felt compelled to buy it."

Tucked inside the box was a tiny stuffed white cow wearing a purple T-shirt and waving one furry hand in the air. I'm sure if I hadn't grabbed it and hugged it to me, it would have jumped into my arms.

My mom had attended Northwestern University. Their school colors are purple and white. I have a photograph of her in a purple sweatshirt and white pants, waving one fist in the air in celebration of Northwestern's football team's rare season of success.

I never dreamed I'd get to hug you again, I thought as I held that silly little creature close to my heart.

"One hundred percent," I could hear Mom's voice say. It was something she'd said countless times before. "I'm behind you one hundred percent."

Finally, I responded—in a language we both understood. "Celestial moos, Mom. Celestial moos."

—*Jan Henrikson*

Bending, Not Breaking

I lost my brother Mike when I was twenty-one and he was twenty. "Lost." Such an odd word, as though the dead could be found again. Yet, in my brother's case, it seems accurate. I see my brother still. I find him in the wit of our oldest son, the intelligence of the second, and the tenderness of the third, his namesake.

Fourteen months separated my brother's and my births. After our sister was born five years later with Rh factor disease, Mike and I became best buddies, allied against parents who pretended away her awkwardness, her deafness, and her inexplicable temper tantrums and insisted we treat her as absolutely normal.

The last letter I had from Mike saluted me as "*Ma petite soeur*," a double joke, because I, although older, was a foot shorter, and while he was fluent in

French, I had just failed my second attempt (we were allowed only three) at passing a required French exam for my graduate degree. Already engaged to be married, I was trying to finish in nine months, before the wedding. In the letter, he'd asked for my help in convincing our parents not to send our sister, then fourteen, to visit him at Princeton, where they expected him to treat her as a date, introducing her to all his friends, taking her to football games, dining with her at his club. My intervention was successful; she did not go.

Less than a month after this letter, my brother died in the early hours of Palm Sunday, but I had no idea. That morning, my housemate had suggested brunch after services at Stanford Memorial Chapel. As we ate in a mall restaurant, a bird flew into the room and darted madly across the ceiling, seeking the skies so clearly visible through the windows. I watched it curiously, but Sandra shuddered.

"A bird in the house means death," she said.

How skillfully I laughed her out of her superstition.

Later that day, I found our brunch had been a ruse to keep me away from the house, where we shared the second floor, because our other house-mate and the landlady had planned a surprise bridal shower for me. I'd just finished opening my gifts when my fiancé called. He stumbled through the details of the accident. Floodwaters crashing through a poorly constructed earthen dam had swept the Volkswagen my brother and his friends traveled in off a country road and into a reservoir.

I couldn't believe Mike was dead because his body hadn't been found and his three friends all had escaped. Why not Mike? Why couldn't he be clinging to a tree somewhere, awaiting rescue?

Nevertheless, I let Sandra make plane reservations while I packed, and I accepted the useless sleeping pills someone brought from the infirmary. Dressed in black, I took a 2:00 A.M. flight out of San Francisco and arrived in Tulsa around noon the next day. I was met by my fiancé, who cried as he told me that Mike's bruised and battered body had been recovered from the water. They say I was strong. My mother says I never cried. I remember trying to get her to eat, being a polite hostess to my sorority sisters who fumbled awkward condolences, thanking my parents' church friends for love expressed in casseroles and gelatin salads, and relaxing only briefly in the comfort of my soon-to-be husband.

I also remember sitting stiff-backed, not weeping, in my pastel Easter suit and hat (my mother insisting on no black), through interminable church services. As an example of Christian strength to the congregation, we attended Maundy Thursday service, Good

Friday service, and, after Mike's Saturday funeral, the Easter Sunday service—a family professing a faith I no longer believed.

My ostensible strength was superficial, brittle. I was a hollow tree trunk surrounding a column of air. An upright object that remained vertical only by grace. A rigid but fragile pillar incapable of bending in my storm of grief, for to do so would only break me in two.

So I did not bend. For the next few months, the rites of mourning absorbed me. I withdrew from university and moved back home to care for my parents and sister. I accompanied them to Princeton to collect my brother's belongings and to attend memorial services there. I wasted time in a do-nothing job at my mother's office so I could keep an eye on her. Then I, still the strong one, married and returned to California and graduate school.

Twenty-five years later, our Mike, our youngest son, rigid with anger and dealing with an alcohol addiction, isolated himself from his father and me. For months, I endured sleepless nights, unanswered letters, and unreturned phone calls from this most tender-hearted of our three boys. I sat in his room, looking at his drawings and paintings, listening to his tapes, embracing the clothes he left behind, wondering if he would ever wear them again. When the pain grew too heavy to bear, when I thought it would break me, I sought therapy.

There, surprisingly, the therapist insisted I first work through my feelings about my brother, his life, and especially, his death. When I was able to release the anger I'd carried because my brother Mike left me too soon and the guilt I felt for somehow not being able to prevent his death, I could finally bend under the weight of my grief over his loss. Then, I could marshal the strength to save the son named for the brother I could not rescue, even if I had been there on that lonely country road with him.

—SuzAnne C. Cole

Floating Questions, Holding Life

arbi is the youngest of four children. She has been known to sign her name with a heart instead of a dot over the i. I am the older of two children, and my name is Kelly with a y. Darbi is short but stout. I am gangly with plain features, easily lost in a crowd.

We lived in the same town, went to the same church, and attended the same college. Opposite in many ways, we made an odd pair. It wasn't until later in life that we discovered that we were more similar than opposite.

Darbi's mom became ill with flu symptoms on a Saturday in January. She was diagnosed with a rare blood disease. She was admitted into the hospital in May and was released for her funeral at the end of that month.

By Christmas, Darbi unexpectedly became pregnant. She was excited by the thought of a new life, a child to carry on her family's legacy. I discovered that I was pregnant at about the same time. We shared all the joys and pains of pregnancy: baby kicks, swollen feet, the ability to eat whatever you want, and heartburn.

I reached seven months of pregnancy before I gave birth to my little boy, prematurely. On the same day, Darbi gave birth at eight months to a little girl.

"Are you ready to see him?" my husband Jeff asked, pushing a wheelchair into my hospital room.

I nodded. I bathed and changed into a crisp hospital gown for the first time in three days. Three days of fighting my way out of toxemia. Three days since my son had been born.

"How does he look?" I asked.

"Beautiful." Jeff bounced with energy, the purple under his eyes the only clue to the stress of the last week.

We arrived at a locked door. Jeff picked up a phone mounted underneath a security camera. "We're here to see our baby, Aaron Wilson," he said.

We held our neon orange hospital bracelets up to the camera, and a nurse buzzed the door open.

Jeff wheeled me through a hallway and past a sign-in desk to a sink station.

After Jeff demonstrated the scrubbing regimen and I followed suit, he wheeled me through another door into a sea of curtained cubicles. Each pastel-colored curtain was attached to a metal track suspended from the ceiling; the curtain could be pulled to enclose the entire area for more privacy. All I could see were ankles and feet and the bottoms of various equipment stands, recliners, and rocking chairs.

The room was neatly partitioned into rows of two cubicles across, each identified by an animal or insect. We rolled up to an Isolette about halfway down the butterfly row. The Isolette reminded me of space paraphernalia from science fiction movies. It sat on a roll-cart about chest-high. Red numbers, similar to an alarm clock, blazed out the temperature of the environment inside its thick hood of clear plastic. My baby lay inside, on display, so close but unreachable.

"Right on time," a nurse whispered from the cubicle on the left. "It's time for him to eat."

"All right!" Jeff whispered, pulling out our video camera. "Pictures?"

"Sure."

When she clicked open the hood of the Isolette, I expected to hear a "whoosh!" The hood stood open, and the nurse gently changed our son's diaper. I heard Aaron squeak in protest, a whisper of a cry. I craned my neck to watch while the nurse swaddled him, my right hand clutching my chest.

"When you hold him," she explained, "make sure his head is back a bit and his chin is up in the air; it helps keep his airway open."

I nodded as she laid his head in the crook of my left arm. Aaron was no bigger around than the arm that cuddled him. I could barely feel his weight of two and a half pounds. He slept with the face of a shriveled, wizened old man. Only the monitor assured me that he was still alive.

Beautiful? I thought. *There is nothing beautiful about this. This was not the way having a baby was supposed to happen. He was too small, too frail. Surely this baby would not live.*

After a week in the hospital, I was finally allowed to go home. I rolled down the window of the car and directed the side mirror on the passenger side so that, as we drove away, I could watch the third-floor windows of the NICU, where my baby lay sleeping in his Isolette, alone.

When we got home, I went to the computer and signed on to the Internet, but felt overwhelmed as I sifted through our e-mail inbox. Instead of reading it all, I opened a new, blank e-mail and began typing a message.

"Whatcha doin?" Jeff asked. He stood behind me, rubbing my shoulders.

"Just sending an e-mail to people, letting them know."

"Oh, well, who are you sending it to?" he said hesitantly.

I turned to face him, confused by his tone. "You know, people we know."

He sighed and sat next to me, holding my hand.

"What?" I asked.

"Well, you should probably know before you send it," he said.

I looked at him, eyebrows raised.

"When I was making phone calls last week, I learned that Darbi was also in the hospital."

"Really?" I asked. My heart beat faster.

"And I found out that her baby . . . died."

"Oh," I said. "Why?"

"They don't know."

I faced the computer and deleted her address from the e-mail message.

"It's a balcony day?" Jeff asked, driving into the church parking lot.

"Definitely."

We were intentionally late for church. I wanted to test my limits, and I had pushed Jeff into taking me to church. We snuck up the stairs into the balcony's dim comfort. We had missed much of the music part of the service. I usually loved to sing, but I couldn't stand the pain, physically or emotionally, of trying. We had arrived in time for the last song, which was enough to dissolve me into tears.

I stared at the cross, hanging high above the stage. I thought of my near death and about Aaron. I picked out the faces of people who had brought us meals or sent us encouraging cards, trying to comfort. I thought about some of their comments: "You've been so blessed." "God has blessed you so much with Aaron." "What a miracle; it's just a miracle."

Blessed? I didn't feel blessed. I had a gouge in my belly; I still couldn't walk very well; my blood pressure remained off the charts; I wasn't producing any breast milk; and my son was currently captive in the NICU. The only time I could see or touch him was during my twice daily one-hour trips to the hospital, the purpose of which was really to deliver measly amounts of breast milk I had managed to squeeze from my uncooperative breasts since my last visit.

I thought about Darbi.

Maybe I was blessed. I was alive. And my baby, though still virtually untouchable, was alive.

But questions continued to turn over in my mind: *What if I hadn't lived and had left my premature son motherless? What if Aaron had died, and instead of worrying and waiting for him to get stronger and for answers, we were, instead, grieving the death of our firstborn child? Would we be blessed then? What if we both had died, leaving Jeff alone and devastated?*

My mind ran over the now-familiar faces of families in the NICU whose babies had been there for months, not weeks, of parents from towns or cities far away who had left jobs and loved ones because this hospital was the only one that could handle their cases. *What about them? Were they blessed? What about Darbi? Was she blessed? Was God punishing all these people but for some reason had overlooked us? Where were their miracles? Where was Darbi's miracle? Were we blessed just because things had gone our way this time?*

Tears dropped onto my hands, folded in my lap.

"I think it's time to go," Jeff whispered.

I nodded and rose to leave.

A refreshing breeze moved puffy clouds through a cornflower blue sky. It was the perfect afternoon for a walk in the park or lounging on a patio, perfect for anything but a funeral for a baby. Darbi's baby.

Pink flowers covered the headstone. Behind the headstone was a barely discernible rectangle cut into the grass, about two feet long by one foot wide. In front of the headstone stood two chairs, covered alternately with darkness and sunlight as evergreens swayed overhead.

I had thought about not coming, worried that my presence would be too upsetting to Darbi, a reminder of how we were opposites once again. But she had called me to say it was all right, that somehow my near tragedy made our friendship possible, that she couldn't really explain it.

People trickled to the graveside. Many of us were old friends; most looked uncomfortable. Was it appropriate to chat? Should we smile at each other? I found myself staring at the headstone, to avoid doing the wrong thing.

The pastor conducting the service directed us to form a wide circle around the gravesite and placed himself opposite the two chairs now holding Darbi and her husband Mike. He held a Bible and wore a tie with a black background and electric-blue swirls. I stared, mesmerized, at the tie; it was not an electric-blue kind of day.

Faced with the difficult task of addressing a group of mourners who wanted not only comfort but also answers—*Why Darbi and Mike? Why Hope?*—the pastor stood with quiet authority and preached a short sermon with an apologetic smile and blue eyes that met each person's in turn. He talked about our various births in life—conception, physical birth, relationships with others, spiritual birth, and rebirth into eternal life. He spoke of how Hope had skipped a few steps, being born into eternal life instead of the physical one. He reminded us that death is not an ending but a beginning.

I had expected the memorial service to provide some validation for Hope's death, of how terrible it was, of how death is a crazy thing that happens to us all. I didn't want spouting about birth phases and eternal life. I wanted assurance that Darbi and I weren't the only ones who felt this terrific pain.

After the sermon, an attendee handed out balloons and markers. We were to write our thoughts to Hope on a balloon and then release it into the beautiful expanse of blue above us. I had no thoughts for Hope. My brain felt frozen. I turned the pink balloon over in my hands, squeaking the rubber beneath my fingertips. Finally, I wrote the only words that came to me, the only words that made sense: "We will remember you." We will remember what it was like to lose you, our pain the black background of our electric-blue joy. We will remember that there are few answers to our questions, the questions that seem to float into that endless expanse of sky.

At Aaron's first birthday party, Darbi laughs and cries at the same time, enchanted by my son and thinking of Hope. She plays with him and reads to him, and her eyes drink him in.

At the end of the day, she holds him as he rests his head against her shoulder, his thumb in his mouth. Holding Aaron, she holds Hope. She holds life.

—*Kelly Wilson*

The Strongest Link

Anne Robinson could not defeat my stepdad, Allan. He wore an eye patch, had lost his hair, and was reclined beneath a checked blanket, drinking weak tea through a straw, but Anne's caustic questions on *The Weakest Link* television show never daunted him. The show's contestants were a team of nine; Allan and I were a solid team of two, our armchairs adjacent, our tactics an unspoken agreement.

At 5:15 P.M., before the national news and while my daughter Katy was at dance class in the church across the street, we'd take our front-row seats in the living room and go head-to-head with Ms. Robinson's one-liners and her nervous guests. My mother would loiter nearby, fussing over Allan, making tea, pulling his cover up over his body, but we'd shoo her away.

"Who has been diagnosed with terminal ignorance?" Anne Robinson demanded of a particularly dismal team one rainy afternoon.

Allan laughed and shook his head, agreeing that they were a moronic bunch.

His diagnosis had never been ignorance, only cancer, a far heavier sentence, but one he fought with dignity. He'd won the battle once before, but the war still challenged him. The vicious tumor in his throat and neck had been conquered by months of chemotherapy and by Allan's resilience. Now, it was back, spreading to his eye and brain. Never grumbling about the pain, he tried to read his favorite *Scott of the Antarctic* books, too proud to ask us to do it for him, and watched TV until he could barely hear the words, all sounds muffled now by the expanding mass in his throat and ear.

Allan and I loved to laugh at the contestants who endured the walk of shame when they were voted off *The Weakest Link* by the rest of the team.

"That half-wit never stood a bloomin' chance," Allan would say, beating Anne Robinson to the punch.

I'd agree. "Who doesn't know that the capital of Bulgaria is Sofia," I'd say, even though I'd thought it was Budapest.

We, of course, would *never* have been voted off. Between us, we had all the answers. What I didn't know, Allan did, and vice versa. What neither of us knew, we chanced.

In the "head–to-head" at the end of the game show, two guests would fight for the big money prize. Whoever got five green ticks first was the victor. Allan always beat them both. He'd suck his tepid tea, never grumbling that his throat hurt or that his eye was irritated from watching television for half an hour, and without needing any sort of buzzer to provide Anne with her answer.

I wrote a long letter to Anne, telling her about Allan's enjoyment of the show, his refusal to let her win, and his equally determined battle with cancer. She sent a signed photograph. Her bold squiggle read, "Keep fighting, Allan." He cried when I presented it to him, in a bronze frame. He insisted it stand on top of the TV and shouted at anyone who tried to move it. It was lifted once a week to be polished by the eternally house-proud Allan and put back in the exact same spot. If my mother moved it when opening a curtain or shifting the TV to get to the plug, he would wordlessly put it back, in the center, pride of place.

"Tell me when we've won," Allan said toward the end of that season of *The Weakest Link*, when he could only stay awake for ten minutes and had no interest in his cup of tea and straw.

I wasn't sure I could play the game without his input. Questions about the war and the nineteenth century fazed me, but I didn't have the heart to rouse him for an answer. I'd guess, but I didn't seem to be as lucky with my choices when I did it alone.

When it was all over and the news started, Allan would open his one good eye and ask, "Did we win?"

"Of course," I'd say. "We got four thousand pounds this time."

We always won. He had beaten cancer the first time, and I was sure he could do it again.

Anne Robinson was at his memorial service, glaring at guests from her spot on top of the TV, the dust on the frame a sure sign that Allan was gone. Family and friends gathered in the living room, their images reflected in the glass that covered Anne's sneer, remembering Allan in their own way, their voices low.

Earlier, as we'd filed down the church aisle behind his coffin, I remembered Anne's show-opening words, "One of you, quite rightly, is about to leave with nothing." She was wrong; Allan had definitely left the victor.

We always leave with something. It might not be what we expect, not a large cash prize or the right answer, but everything leaves its mark. I am left with all my memories of my stepdad, my true dad, my Allan. I am left with photographs of him camping, of him smiling with my mother in front of his beloved RV, of him with his children and grandchildren, of him planting flowers in the garden.

I still watch *The Weakest Link*, but I struggle now to answer all the questions. I could cheat, get out the encyclopedia or ask my husband or son. I could turn it off, but I find I'm unable. Something in Anne's scathing presence comforts me. Sometimes, I think I can hear Allan whispering the answers in my ear, the history and the general-knowledge ones that we wordlessly agreed he would take care of, while I covered literature and the arts. Perhaps I knew the answers all along. Perhaps I just enjoyed seeing him fight and ultimately win. And perhaps he did.

As the credits roll and the music plays like the final hymn at his funeral, I imagine Anne's voice closing the show as it should. "Allan, you are the strongest link. Goodbye."

—*Louise Beech*

Her House Was in Order

On the night before my mother died, I was down on my knees scrubbing her pale beige living room carpeting. She was in the next room, tethered to oxygen, drifting in and out of consciousness.

For weeks, my world and hers had been her one-bedroom apartment. I had come to know every inch of that limited space, every shadow that fell as the light changed, every accessory and photograph in her contained world.

While my mother spun out of control medically—when her "vitals," as the hospice nurses who tended to her called her blood pressure, respiration, and temperature readings, became indicators of her impending death—only the spots and stains on that beige carpeting seemed capable of being brought into submission.

So I had rummaged in the utility closet of my mother's apartment, looking for a bucket. The one I found was filled with rags and seemed to come from another civilization, as did so many of my mother's worldly goods. It was shallow and made of metal, not plastic. And it was tucked way back in a corner, suggesting that it hadn't had very much use of late.

No wonder. Why would my dying, ninety-seven-year-old mother need or use a bucket? The sudden realization that all domesticity was so far behind her made me stand at that closet and gasp at the renunciations of this final chapter of my mother's life. Once, she had been a superlative housekeeper, the kind who could sweep, bake, and tend to children without ever losing her focus or her way.

Terminal illness and the caprices of a body grown old and punishing had changed it all. I wondered whether the soil in her wall-to-wall living room carpeting had bothered Mom, despite her failing vision. It was too late to ask . . . but not too late to set things right.

In my rummaging for a scrub brush that might work some of the soil out of those carpet fibers, I came upon other retired supplies: the clothespins from her other life in the suburbs, carried to this urban one decades ago; a collection of half-empty bottles of disinfectants that smelled of pine; and, behind almost everything else, the kind of chamois cloth I remembered from my childhood. Does anybody use chamois cloths anymore? Or do they hide, like a guerilla army, in the backs of closets of old, once-perfect housekeepers like my mother?

That night, when the only sound in the apartment was the constant hum of the oxygen tank in my mother's bedroom, I lined up my ammunition. Scrub bucket, brush, liquid detergent, rags fashioned from Mom's old flannel nightgowns, and a touch of ammonia. I rolled up the legs of my corduroy pants and got to work. I scrubbed the foamy bubbles from that bucket in ever-widening circles, not sticking to a pattern, but working almost randomly, until my forearms ached. Then I would pause, look at the promising results, and scrub some more. In the end, it wasn't just the spots I was after. It was every inch of carpet. Somehow, this scrubbing had taken on a ferocity that felt almost primal and sacred.

And that's how I spent one long evening as my mother lay dying. For as long as I scrubbed, I could control something. As the spots and grime rubbed out and the living room began smelling of lemons and ammonia, the terrible sadness lifted and life seemed almost normal—if normal includes stopping to feed my mother pudding from a spoon and checking that her emaciated body was comfortable in her rented hospital bed.

In the face of the surreal, the real becomes the Holy Grail. And cleaning is about as real as it gets.

After I'd scrubbed the carpeting, I began a cleaning binge that might have appeared demonic to an eyewitness. As Mom slept fitfully, I flung open the kitchen cabinets and began sorting out the contents. Old cereal boxes went, along with outdated canisters of bread crumbs and the pretzels that Mom once loved but that had grown mealy and stale.

I worked in a certain frenzied rhythm in the silent apartment, where no TV offered that familiar white-noise background and no phones rang anymore. Friends had stopped calling to ask solicitously, "How is she today?" That suited me just fine; I was weary of saying, "No change. She's very weak."

On that night, the cleaning gave me purpose in the silence. I worked until I was bone tired, the kind of tired that almost guarantees a night of sleep. I sorted and wiped and polished and dusted. I even cleaned the TV screen with a mix of ammonia and water, only to find I'd made it streaky. The defeat felt so monumental that I wept.

But I'd learned, through the process of my mother's dying, that tears spill out for reasons other than the apparent ones. I wasn't crying over streaks on the TV screen; I was crying over what had happened in a few short months to the charming, high-spirited, happy woman in the hospital bed in her yellow bedroom. This room, once filled with light and life, was now a dispensary for pill bottles and potions; a jumble of notes and logs recording her vitals, her food and liquid intake, her medications, and various other details on her deteriorating condition; and those inserts that come with medicines and outline the potential dire consequences of swallowing them. I wanted to sweep all of it—all the bottles and tubes and papers—off my mother's dresser and night table. I wanted to toss every last disturbance in the field into some vast incinerator. But that would come later.

The last thing I did the night before my mother died was to clean out the hall closet. Closet purges have always been the closest thing to redemption I know. Organizing the coats and gloves, hats and scarves that Mom would never wear again seemed like a touchstone to her once orderly life. Even though she would never see the clothing on hangers neatly arranged, the scarves neatly folded, and each glove nestled with its mate, I had to believe that she somehow knew that everything was in its proper place and that her home had been restored to the condition in which she had always kept it.

My mother died as the sun was setting the next day. Outside, the world went on. Horns blared, sirens screamed, and on the sidewalk, twenty-five stories down, people were leaving work and heading home. So was my mother, the superb housekeeper. And her house was in order.

—*Sally Friedman*

Not Good at Goodbyes

Only a heartbeat ago, it seems, I was the younger generation, shielded from inevitability by parents and grandparents. They were loving people who tolerated, even ignored, my mistakes and indulged my reluctance to grow up. I wished time away with reckless abandon; there would always be more. But the years passed, all too quickly, and my grandparents and then my parents died. I was now the older generation. Now, I understood the inevitabilities of life . . . and death.

Aunt Charlotte and Uncle Jack remained as buffers to my mortality after the loss of my parents, and I clung to their presence in my life. When Charlotte became ill suddenly, I panicked. She would get better, I reasoned in a moment of calm. I refused to acknowledge that she might be leaving me. One afternoon, I dreamed I was in her hospital room.

"Is that who I think it is?" she said, and her eyes told me that it meant the world to her that I was there.

"It's me, Auntie," I said. "I'm here."

My dream came as no surprise. I thought of Charlotte constantly while awake, so why shouldn't she be in my dreams, too? I wondered if the dream meant that she knew how much I wanted to be with her. If I stretched my imagination far enough, if I went back to a time when I believed anything was possible, maybe I could believe I was really there.

Four thousand miles and more money than I possessed prevented my dream from becoming a reality. I longed to phone my aunt on Sunday at five o'clock, just like I did every week. We'd laugh because my card had arrived before her birthday for the first time in years. But even that was not possible. When my cousin Marion, Charlotte and Jack's niece, called to tell me her mother was dying—that "it's only a matter of time now"—I knew there would be no more Sunday phone calls, no more conversations that left me smiling and feeling secure.

During my wait for that final call from Marion, I tortured myself with remembrance, losing myself in

a slideshow of images. Outside my windows, everything looked frigid and bleak. Winter had put the
world to sleep, creating a fitting landscape for my
feelings. No brilliant sunshine to mock me. No perfect, cloudless sky to discount my sorrow.

I had always wanted Charlotte and Jack to see
our farm. So many times I'd pictured the three of
us driving over the hill—the big one just before
getting to our place. I would watch their faces
carefully as they saw the dignified brick house surrounded by acres of peanuts, soybeans, and cotton
for the first time. They'd see the red outbuildings,
the post-and-rail fencing, and the rooster stealing
cat food from the bowl on the back porch. Charlotte would say, "It's really lovely, dear." They'd be
so happy for me.

As a child, I'd wished that I would live on a farm
when I grew up. Maybe wishes did come true. Now, I
wished Aunt Charlotte wouldn't leave me. I wished
for years and years more to spend with her, for dozens of visits to my farm.

We'd marvel over the glossy green magnolia tree
in the front yard and the twisted ancient sycamore
in the back. I'd show them where the floodwaters
stopped their frightening crawl up our driveway
after the hurricane. We'd shake our heads and smile,
because, with time, some things become worthy of

amusement and wonder. Losing her would never be anything but painful.

I'm sure Aunt Charlotte knew I loved her. I told her countless times. The abiding love of a small child grew to include deep respect and admiration. With the clarity that sometimes comes only with loss, though, I now wonder if she knew how much she meant to me and how much I learned from her. She taught me to believe in myself. She taught me that there's no sin in making mistakes and that everyone deserves another chance.

Every summer and holiday, when I stayed with my aunt and uncle on their farm in southern Alberta, Canada, I became their little girl. I watched Aunt Charlotte with Uncle Jack, and I learned about love and devotion. I watched her work endless hours for endless days, and I learned about commitment. I watched her with friends and family, and I learned about loyalty. When hail destroyed an ocean of gold wheat—their entire crop—on a blistering August afternoon, she held me tight and told me everything was going to be okay. That's when I learned about faith and perseverance.

When it was time to leave the farm and return to my family in the city, I always cried. Our time together never lasted long enough. I was never very good at saying goodbye. I'm still not.

I found out later that Aunt Charlotte died at the same time I dreamed of her—at the moment I touched her cheek and whispered, "It's me, Auntie. I'm here."

—*Susan B. Townsend*

A version of this story, titled "Saying Goodbye," was first published in The Rose & Thorn *literary e-zine, spring 2004.*

Heading Home

My husband George and I returned to our quiet house after one of his chemotherapy sessions. He immediately walked over to the television and turned it on.

"Dodgers are playing today," he said with a tired smile. I marveled at how the mention of his Dodgers always perked him up, even though he was exhausted from chemotherapy. "Come watch it with me," he patted the sofa.

At one time I would have passed on his invitation, because I didn't like baseball. Not now. I smiled and sat next to him.

We were newlyweds, young and madly in love, when George said he had a surprise for me. I couldn't imagine what it would be. A special dinner? A favorite play? He held up two tickets.

"We're going to a Dodgers' game." He flashed me a mischievous grin.

My heart sank. I knew my husband loved baseball, especially the Dodgers. I tried to work up interest, but I couldn't get excited about men hitting a ball and running around the bases. I found it boring. Even though he suspected I wasn't much of a baseball fan, I knew he wanted to win me over.

"Oh, good," I said half-heartedly, trying to sound excited and not quite succeeding.

"The games are going to be held in the L.A. Coliseum until their new stadium is built. I can't wait."

I could. He walked away, happier than a kid on Christmas morning.

A week later, we walked into the coliseum, nicknamed "home run heaven" because it was supposedly easier to hit a home run in their temporary venue. George nodded toward the field after we found our seats. "Look, honey, there they are." His eyes sparkled as he watched the Dodgers run out onto the field, their blue and white uniforms gleaming in the afternoon sun.

I watched the game disinterested. I didn't have a clue what was happening during the innings. I found myself drifting off, thinking about other things, but George was totally focused on the game. Every so often, he would grab my hand in excitement when a batter got a hit. I smiled, trying to show enthusiasm, but between hits, my mind continued to drift off. To me, the only fascinating thing about baseball was singing "Take Me Out to the Ball Game" during the seventh-inning stretch.

The second time we went to see the Dodgers, I found George's excitement to be contagious. When I asked him some questions about the game, his face brightened. I could see he was pleased that I showed interest, so he tried to explain the various plays. Much of the fun in watching, he explained, was anticipating the plays. If the batter gets a hit with a runner at third, they can score. If he gets a good bunt, a runner at second can make it to third and so on. He even tried to explain the "infield fly rule." By that time, my head was spinning.

I smiled at his enthusiasm as he continued on. "But the best is always bases loaded, nobody out. That's the best—the ideal situation. Nothing is better than that."

I could see he wanted me to appreciate the game as much as he did; he wanted that so much. But I still wasn't sold.

Soon, his team got their own stadium. George proudly marched into the Dodgers' new home as if he owned it. The reddish brown dirt surrounding the perfectly mowed green grass, the warm California weather, and the excited fans anticipating a great game all added up to a memorable day.

During one magic moment of the game, George nudged me and nodded toward the field. "Honey, look," he said excitedly, "bases are loaded, nobody out."

The ideal situation. I moved to the edge of my seat. Now, I understood.

The Dodgers didn't let us down. With a loud *crack!*, the batter hit one into the stands.

From then on, I was a staunch baseball fan. George and I would sit in the stands, munching on "Dodger dogs," eating Cracker Jacks and peanuts, listening to the roar of the crowd, and cheering our team on. When we couldn't be at the games, we listened on the radio to the soothing voice of Vin Scully calling the plays.

Our family grew to include three children, who matured and married and gave us eight grandchildren. Over the years, any number of us would attend games together. Time passed quickly and brought many changes, but the Dodgers remained constant.

Then, shortly after George and I celebrated our forty-third wedding anniversary, George became ill. An X-ray showed a shadow on his lungs, which turned out to be cancer. After going through surgery, he started chemotherapy and radiation. He remained positive throughout his illness, and we never doubted that the treatment would be successful.

Unfortunately, that was not the case. We got a second opinion that twisted my stomach into knots. Even though the treatment had slowed the tumor's growth, it was a recurring cancer. It would be back.

By late summer, George had become weaker and could no longer attend the Dodgers games in person, but whenever he could, he watched the games on television. Occasionally, a friend of the family, a Franciscan priest, would drop by to visit. He and George would sit and visit for hours, talking about many things, but we both knew that our dear friend was helping my husband make his peace with God. It was a comfort to both George and me.

One day, when George went for a doctor's appointment because he was having trouble breathing, we were shocked to see his chest X-ray. It showed a very fast-growing tumor. The doctor put him in the hospital immediately.

It was four days before Thanksgiving. We discussed him coming home for the holiday, but the doctors said they would be unable to control the pain. They told us the end was near.

I walked through the next couple of days feeling as if I existed with half a heart. Like a robot, I put one foot in front of the other, not thinking, numb.

Family and friends crowded in to see George. Once, when a pastor from my daughter's church visited, I overheard my husband tell him he was getting ready to go home.

I turned to my oldest daughter and said, "He knows he can't go home. Why—?" Then I stopped. Realizing what he'd meant my eyes filled with tears.

The doctors put George on a morphine drip. Over the next couple of days, he would mumble occasionally and I would lean over trying to hear what he was saying. I struggled to hear every word.

Exactly four days after Thanksgiving, George startled us when he sat, bolt upright, in the bed. "Bases . . . " he said softly.

Our children, standing around his bedside, heard it, too.

"What, honey?" I asked. "Bases . . . ?"

Very faintly, he said, "Bases loaded, nobody out." Then he lay back down.

We all looked at each other. My heart swelled as I realized what he was saying. Slowly, a smile spread across my face as I repeated the phrase. "Bases loaded, nobody out."

A short time later, my husband left this world.

There was a time when that phrase meant nothing to me; now, it gave me great comfort. In his final moments, my husband had reached out to connect with me again in a special way. If, many years before, I hadn't opened myself up to a sport he loved, I wouldn't have been able to share in his finest hour—when, with no outs and bases loaded, the ideal situation for a home run, he swung the bat, connected with the ball, rounded the bases, and headed for home.

—Mary Lou Reed

A version of this story was first published in The Daily Breeze, *April 2008.*

Winks from Heaven

Her name was Juliette Veronica. Perhaps, out of respect, her children and grandchildren should have called her Momma and Nana, respectively. But she was Googie to everybody.

"My baby brother, John, called me that, when he couldn't say 'Julie,'" she would say. "Sure and it's been Googie from then on. And that is that!"

Born on the Fourth of July of Irish immigrant parents, this dark-haired spitfire with opalescent eyes who stood all of four-feet-something was a proud first-generation American who wore her birthday like a badge of honor. She was just as proud of her Celtic heritage and the Emerald Isle. She danced and swayed to the tune of flute music no one else heard as she mopped floors and scraped dishes, singing slightly off-key in a voice too big for her slight body. When she was on her knees in her tiny vegetable garden, coaxing peas and peppers and fresh parsley to life, the strains of "H- A- double R- I- G- A- N spells Harrigan . . ." drifted up into the air above her and out the window, carried on the wind and over the neighbors' fences. If you looked closely enough, you would swear the fairies were dancing in circles around her. Googie was *magic.*

"Come over here with you, my gal!" My grandmother caught me peeking from behind the lilac bushes and smiled. She cupped my too-round cheeks in her grimy hands. "You've got your father's face."

"And your baby brother John's, too, Googie!" I shrieked. Googie's eyes twinkled. Laughing, she wiped garden dust from my face with her apron corner.

"That you do, my gal. That you do."

I didn't meet Googie—not officially, anyway—until the day of my mother's funeral, when I was six. Until then, I knew only her cheerful, lilting voice on the long-distance wire, and her many letters, which I scrambled often to the mailbox to collect. Printed in green ink, the letters were full of grand stories and meticulously drawn cartoon figures. Until the day of my mother's death, Googie was a happy fantasy, surrounded in my wishful child's eye by shamrocks and fairy dust.

It was so cold at the cemetery that December day that my feet felt frozen to the ground. Midway through the service, fresh snow began to swirl downward, dusting my mother's coffin. My father reached forward to brush it off, releasing his grip on my mittened hand. From almost nowhere, the warm grasp of a tiny, smiling lady took his place. I had never seen her before, but I knew right away who she was from her pictures in the mail. The snow wisping and eddying around her face looked every bit like fairy dust.

"Come with Googie, my gal. We have things to do."

That first day blended and blurred into night. Adults came and went, speaking in whispers. When it was dark and the house was still, my father and grandfather sat in Googie's parlor and were quiet. I wiped hot tears and sniffled. My grandmother whisked my coat and mittens from the hall tree. Bundling me up, she yanked a hankie trimmed in Irish lace from her pocket, sniffling into it herself.

"Come on out with you. Googie's got something to show you."

The snow had stopped, and in the moonlight, the frozen sidewalks glistened.

"It's pretty, isn't it?" Googie asked.

I shrugged, still feeling cold, filled with a nagging emptiness.

My grandmother stood there for a moment, biting her bottom lip. Then, as if on a whim, she lifted me up and pointed to the clear night sky. Looking into me with clear, piercing, light-gray eyes, she placed her hand on my chin and said, "Look up. It's a fine sight, it is."

Although I didn't want to, I couldn't help it. All above us, the stars shone like diamonds in the midnight-blue sky. It was beautiful, but I felt very small.

"You know, my gal, in Ireland they say that the stars are forever. See how bright they are? They are as bright tonight as when your father was your age and when I was your age. The stars will always be there."

I began to listen.

"And do you know why they shine so? They do because, every night, they have a party in heaven, to welcome the new souls who come back to God. They twinkle and glow to light the way home."

"That's just a story," I muttered.

"Oh no, my gal. 'Tis the truth. When I was a young girl, just about your size, my little brother John was awfully sick. There was nothing the doctor could do. I sat by his bed and I was very sad, like you are now. Right before he closed his eyes for the last time, he opened them wide, like saucers, and he smiled a big, big smile, just about like yours."

In spite of myself, a smile erupted across my face.

Googie went on. "He was so pale, but his face, it lit up almost like the fireworks on the Fourth of July. 'Googie,' he said to me, 'the stars are blinking and winking for me. They are so warm. Can you feel them?' Of course, I couldn't. Then he told me, 'Tonight, Googie, look for the brightest star in the sky, and that will be me.'"

My grandmother crouched down and held me close, pointing upward again. "My gal, John did just as he promised, and I knew he had made it to heaven," Googie said. "Now, you look up there and find the brightest star winking. That would be your mother, waving down and telling you the very same thing."

We stayed at Googie's house until I was almost grown. That was a long time ago. The last I heard, lilac bushes still perfume the breeze in her old garden, even though different hands now churn the rich soil and the fairies no longer dance in happy circles 'round the pepper plants. At least, I don't think they do. You can never tell, though.

But from where I am now, far from Googie's garden and my childhood home, when I go for my evening walk, I can still find the brightest star. And it always winks at me, while all the other stars around it always look, for the life of me, like fairy dust, dancing in the night to the tune of flutes that only Googie and I can hear.

—Candy Killion

The Part That Stays

The year my son Ethan was in kindergarten, I lost both my parents to cancer. My father died on May 20, a week after Mother's Day and exactly one week before he would have turned eighty-four. The combination of Mother's Day, my father's birthday, and the anniversary of his death makes May a painful month for me. Then, when it's over, there's still Father's Day to face.

I miss being somebody's daughter. I miss the sense of safety that comes only from parental love. My dad was fiercely protective. I moved about my world secure in the belief that he "had my back." Yet, in all honesty, it wasn't always easy being his child. The first few times my father held Ethan as a baby he grew tearful.

"Those eyes are staying blue," he said when Ethan was three weeks old. "What a gorgeous guy. I can't get over how good looking this kid is." I had to agree with him. Ethan really was a beautiful baby.

Still, it stung when he added, "No one in my family was ever this good looking."

Years before, when I'd first introduced Dad to the man who would eventually become Ethan's father, he said Richard was too handsome for me. He went on to tell me the story of his ugly distant cousin who married a very attractive man and how the marriage had ended in divorce. That time, I'd cried long and hard after he left, then cried again the next day in my therapist's office.

"I'm pretty, aren't I?"

"Very." My therapist handed me a tissue so I could blow my runny nose.

"So why doesn't my own father think so?"

I have cerebral palsy, a disability that causes me to walk with a limp. She believed it had to do with that. "The damage is physical, so when your father appraises you, he doesn't see a perfect-looking girl."

It made sense, but still, it bothered me.

"So he focuses on how smart you are," she went on to say. "There are worse things."

It is true that my father was proud of me, and he was clearly proud of Ethan, too. Taking a breath, I did my best to shrug off his comment, but in the throes of what I now realize were postpartum blues, I felt too sensitive to let it go. With a bulging blob for a belly and hair that hadn't been combed twice since

I'd become a mother, I was sure I really did favor my father's ugly distant cousin, at least for the moment. So, when he persisted in fussing over Ethan's good looks, I reacted by teasing him.

"I think he resembles you," I said.

He straightened a little in his chair. "Really?"

"Sure." Feeling only slightly guilty, I added, "You know how it is with babies and balding old men."

Moments like those are painful to look back on after someone is gone. A few times, when Ethan (now twelve) has said something particularly cutting to me, I've caught myself warning him about such regrets. "How will you feel if that's the last thing you say to me?" But making Ethan feel guilty doesn't help either of us. Our children show us their worst selves because they need a safe place to let out those emotions. Doing so helps them face the harder, less forgiving parts of their lives. Absorbing our kids' anger and bruised feelings is not the easiest aspect of parenting, but I was fortunate enough to learn that it's not the hurtful words we hold on to in the end.

I spent the first Mother's Day after my mom's death beside my father's hospital bed. I'd been visiting him regularly during the previous weeks, and each time I'd seen him, he was less and less himself.

Shortly after I arrived that Sunday, he said to me, "I want you back."

"Who?" I asked, thinking he must be confusing me with someone else, some lost love, maybe even my mother. But then he said my name: "Ona."

"I'm right here," I told him, taking his hand.

"Really?" he asked, with wonder in his eyes.

A nurse came in to take his vitals. My father had a look of deep feeling on his face that could have easily been mistaken for pain.

"Talk to me, Leonard," the nurse said. "What's the matter?"

"I love this girl so much," he answered.

"What girl, Dad?" I asked. Again he said "Ona."

"Me? Your daughter?"

He nodded. "I should have noticed you sooner."

That's when I realized that the details of exactly how we were connected no longer mattered. In this last phase of life, context wasn't necessary. Certainly, any harsh words or hard moments between us over the years were forgotten—were, in fact, beside the point. All he knew was that he loved me. All that was left was love.

We looked into each other's eyes and nodded. Silently, we were making a pact. I would be here for him. I would be here to receive this great love.

His lunch arrived, and I helped him eat. His hand shook as he lifted a Styrofoam cup of tea to his lips, so I laid my hand on top of his to keep the hot liquid from spilling. His fingers felt dry and cool. Carefully, he took a drink and then kissed my hand, over and over, punctuating each sip with another kiss.

That was the last time he was able to speak to me. When I visited the next Sunday, I knew I'd never see him alive again. He had that particular distant gaze I recognized from my mother that meant he was already leaving. Still, he lifted his hand to tell me he wanted it held. I did the talking. I thanked him for his solidity and generosity, told him I would miss him and was scared, but I also assured him that I'd be all right.

Early the next morning he died. A while after I got the call, I went for a walk. It occurred to me that with my parents gone I had lost my one guaranteed source of unconditional love. But then the breeze tickled the back of my neck the way my father used to do and I knew it wasn't true. Love like that doesn't leave with the body. It's the part that stays. When you're walking alone on the saddest of days, it is love that holds you upright and gets you through.

—Ona Gritz

A version of this story was first published in the online literary journal Literary Mama.

Believe, Persevere, Continue

Every Christmas season I put on a holiday tea for my girlfriends. We are a diverse group of women: mothers, wives, engineers, department heads, administrators, teachers, doctors, artists, and writers. This year we were minus one—my closest writing pal, Linda. She'd planned to be with us. Even after her diagnosis turned terminal, she wrote to tell me she intended to make it to this year's gathering. And I believed her. After all, the first several rounds of chemo and radiation hadn't even taken her hair, she wasn't dropping weight, and her face didn't have that washed-out look that can show up during cancer treatment.

But, as I look back now, I think she knew way more than she shared. A week before my birthday in September, a package arrived. Inside was a Christmas-themed table runner—with a nine-patch quilt square for each end section, and a large middle square with St. Nicholas poised in the center and the word "Believe" bordering all four sides.

Three weeks later, in early October, Linda died.

Linda and I had both left the conventional work world—she, the medical field, and I, the cubicles of corporate America—after our families were grown and gone from home. We decided to spend our days working on creative writing. Every January, Lin and I would each choose a word that would serve as the defining guide for our approach to our writing goals in the coming year. In 2008, she'd chosen "persevere" and I'd chosen "believe."

Several months earlier, before we knew of her cancer diagnosis, I'd ordered her a bracelet, intending to give it to her for her birthday in November. It was an Unexpected Miracles® bracelet threaded with wooden beads that had the Chinese character for "Good Karma" carved into them, alternating with semi-precious agate stones. Agate is a "power" gem for inviting love, courage, and strength to oneself. Paired with good karma, it seemed a fine token to encourage her in her quest to find a literary agent or a publisher for her completed novels. She'd had no luck in obtaining either and at times became discouraged.

We exchanged e-mails daily, first thing in the morning; we'd outline our writing plans for the day and share bits of family news before signing off to get to work. In June, when her morning e-mails started to paint the increasingly grim picture of her illness—the cancer having spread to her brain, making reading and writing increasingly difficult—something told me she needed that bracelet now. Still, I hesitated to send it to her, because I didn't want her to think I was denying the seriousness of her illness. Eventually, though, I listened to my heart and mailed it to her. In a letter I explained what my original intentions had been but told her that now, in light of the metastasized cancer, the bracelet was to bring her the unexpected miracle of each new day.

It was the right thing to do, as the shaky, hand-written note she sent me confirmed: "I am wearing my beads constantly. Your heart could not be more generous. I am looking forward to my dreams and goals and work. I am still here with you."

After lifting the table runner from the gift box that September afternoon, I admired Linda's handi-work and traced the lines of her stitching. I was so touched that she'd made a personal gift for me, especially knowing how difficult it must have been, given the unsteadiness of her hands and the strug-gles within her brain to maneuver a sewing machine.

It couldn't have been more valuable to me had she sewn it with real gold thread. One day, a stranger might examine the wavy line of stitching along the edges and think some amateur made the quilt, but to me the stitching is perfect. It is a testament to an everlasting friendship, to a courageous woman wanting to leave a friend with one final gift—a reminder to believe.

I know Linda wanted me to persist in our mutual dream of writing and then publishing those words, sharing my stories with others. She knew she wasn't going to be around to continue the trek with me, so she wanted to make sure I would persevere, that I would continue believing in my dream.

I'll have that table runner until I no longer need it. My daughters know how special it is to me.

At Christmas, my youngest asked, "Mom, are you sure you even want to use it? What if something gets spilled on it?"

I told her Lin made the runner for me to use. When it needs washing, it will be handled gently, but it will be used. It's one way of keeping Lin around.

Now, every morning when I open up e-mail, I collide head-on with her absence, and at times the thought that I will never again see her name flash up in my in-box is more than I can swallow. I can still see her face, hear her voice, see her eyes when she'd challenge me to "quit trying to be a perfectionist and just send it out! It's time to let it go, Bec.'"

My loneliness for my dear friend is not going to go away easily or quickly, but as I look through my notes and cards tacked to the bulletin board in my office, I realize how much of her is all around me. There are cards of encouragement—the word "believe" is a strong theme for many of them. There are notes from conferences we went to together, thank you notes for friendship in rough times, and just-because notes. And there are pictures of us taken together at last year's holiday tea.

My new motivational word for this year is "continue." Linda would be pleased that I continue to employ the practice she introduced me to—focusing on my word and on my goals for a whole year, striving to make the work take shape and the dream come true. This, among many things, is what she left me.

—Rebecca Groff

Violets Aren't Blue

From my desk I spy a silver-framed photo of my little boy, barely one year old, staring out a window at the marvel of his first snowfall. He is in profile, and the sun's brilliant reflection on the blanket of white outside highlights his red-blond hair, painting the illusion of a halo on the tiny angel wearing an oversized, red Wildcats sweatshirt. A woman bends over him; her hair is gray, and her profile is one I know well: my mother. Her hand rests lovingly on the little boy's head, and her expression of wonder and delight reflects his own. But she's not excited about the snow; she's excited about him.

It was my son's first Christmas away from home, which is California. We had flown back for the holiday to my native Ohio, and my mom, who had all but given up on my ever having a baby, was constantly in awe of the little miracle of my son, Noel. She was the perfect grandma, as she was the perfect mother, a woman for whom the job was the pinnacle of life. I used to resent that. I used to look at her and think, *Why didn't she ever do anything with her life? How can she just want to be a wife and a mother? How can she be content with watering her flowers and making afghans out of colored yarn? I was convinced my dad had talked her into it.*

But that Christmas, when I looked at her looking at Noel, I realized something important: My mother had chosen her role in life, and it was a choice with which she was well satisfied.

I had always been the one in the family who was going to do things. I wanted to be a writer, to get away from Ohio and go to a place over the rainbow, someplace where things were happening and people were thinking and books were important. I knew so much then. I knew that my little hometown was a backwater place with no discernible culture, and that my parents were nice people who didn't know very much, and that the deep faith they held in God and in the basic goodness of people was just a sham, the opiate of the people I had learned about in college. I knew that I'd moved out just in time, before I could get sucked into that stupid contentment that comes with living in one place your whole life.

When my mom went to the store, she always saw somebody she knew. The same lady had cut her hair for nearly forty years, and she had grown up and been baptized by the same priest who eventually said her funeral mass. Her sisters, her mother, her father, the nuns who taught her in Catholic school—nearly all had spent their whole lives in this small-time farm town.

It wasn't until much later in life, when I saw Jimmy Stewart run through the snowy streets of Bedford Falls in the classic film *It's a Wonderful Life,* that I started to appreciate the joy and contentment of sameness. The drive to leave was deep in me, as it is in many people who want to accomplish things. It's difficult to achieve greatness (or so we think) in a place where everyone remembers you as a toddler running naked through a sprinkler in the summer. Still, when I visited that Christmas, I was struck not only by the sameness of this place but also by the beauty in the continuity of my mother's life.

Of course, as a teenager, I didn't see the value of this. I saw a rut where, in reality, there was a deep furrow laid for planting. I saw boring old buildings, where there was actually a fascinating history. I saw naïveté, where, upon closer examination, there was wisdom. I had chosen, at a young age, to leave all of that. And, as they say, you can never go home again . . . except, perhaps, at Christmas.

My family has observed a number of peculiar Christmas traditions for many years—most of them originated by my mother. Mom putting little elf foot-prints on the windowsill to convince us that Santa had, indeed, received our letters. The jangling of a sleigh's bell-laden harness every year at midnight on Christmas Eve, a harness she swore was captured by my grandfather one year when he caught Saint Nick on the roof. My three little sisters and I creating Christ-mas plays with the time-worn fairy ornaments strung from the branches of our tree. Over time, some of the traditions have changed, but they have all stayed with us, and the stories of Christmases past are recounted every year, taken out like an old favorite toy.

Last year, the last holiday we were to have with our mother, we all gathered for Christmas at the home of my sister, the one who lived a mile from my parents' trailer. Her house, inherited when her hus-band's father died, sits on a reservoir and golf course. That day, the view out their front bay window—the landscape dusted with sparkling snow and dotted with occasional sledders—looked like a Currier and Ives painting. The small house was filled with the smells of roast turkey, pies, cinnamon, bread—all the starchy mainstays of a Midwestern holiday feast. The windows were steamed, and the kids drew mis-shapen faces in the condensation as my sister's over-sized dog licked and tore at presents no matter who they were for.

When we met in the great room to open gifts, we all took turns, just as we did when I was a kid. Everybody opened one present, then showed it to everyone else and exclaimed about how great it was, even if it was yet another pair of slippers or a necktie with cows on it, or even, as was the case with my nephew, a pirate costume that was appropriated by his daddy, who walked around with a hook hand all day, trying to spear cookies off peoples' plates. And, of course, there was Mom, hovering over everyone, gathering wrapping paper discards, snapping pictures, cleaning up dirty plates.

"Open a present, Mom," my youngest sister urged her.

With each gift she opened, Mom took a moment to unwrap it as carefully as if she were handling rare artifacts, then exclaimed with authentic delight at yet another pair of slippers or a homemade, lopsided pinch pot, or perfume she probably wouldn't wear. At least one gift usually featured violets, her favorite flower. She probably had the largest collection of violet-patterned dish towels, handkerchiefs, scarves, nightgowns, coffee cups, and blankets in all the Midwest.

It is Christmas again—the first one without Mom—I'm home in surreal California, where the Santas wear Hawaiian shirts and ride surfboards instead of sleighs. Although the joy of the day will not be dimmed, because I know Noel will be so happy about his first set of real drums, deep inside, in a small, dark place I have kept hidden so far today, I feel a sadness, a sense of loss, and a void that cannot be filled by anything.

I awaken early on this Christmas morning, before everyone else, just as my mom used to do. In the sparkle of the tree's lights, I think about her, about how much she would have loved to see the expression on Noel's face when he opens the drums he asked Santa for. Sipping coffee in the dimness of my silent living room, I wait, as she used to wait, for my child to awaken and bring the house to life. A tear slips down my cheek as I recall all the care and love Mom put into making each Christmas special for me and my sisters.

After the amazing morning of presents and music and food, my little family and I are all resting, and I look outside at my little patio. Jasmine plants snake up into the white lattice, but with the recent Santa Ana weather they are dry, so I decide to water them.

My mother never would have let any plant in her garden go dry, I think.

This reminds me of the day of her funeral in June, when we got to my parents' house and I kept noticing that her beloved marigolds and violets were parched but then kept forgetting to water them. That night, I awakened to a raging thunderstorm that dumped inches of water onto the yard. I apologized to my mom for not remembering to water, but as usual, she'd taken care of it herself. I sat on the closed-in porch that dark morning, watching the rivulets of water stream from the streetlight, onto the sidewalks, and into reflecting pools. Wrapped in her blue fleece robe, I huddled into the chair and cried with the rain. That was six months ago. Today, the grief cuts nearly as deep.

People understand grief when it's fresh. But as the months go by, those who've never experienced it figure you should have gotten over it by now, like a nasty bout of the flu. Those who have experienced it know that you never get over it. If grief is a virus, it is one that, although it may go dormant, never leaves you and for which there is no cure. There is only peaceful coexistence. My grief is tamed but not gone. Any small thing can trigger it, and it is the same with my sisters. On Christmas, it's worse. It is the day above all days that I remember her, remember her care and love and the joy she drew from being a mother.

I decide to water my plants. My son is sleeping, so I can leave the house without an escort. I go outside, extricate the hose from its embrace of weeds, and aim it at the pots of poor, dry jasmine, which soak up the moisture gratefully. A few flowers are actually blooming in the side garden under our eternally fruit-bearing orange tree; it is, after all, southern California, and things bloom all year long, something my mother loved. A few African daisies peek out from the dense greenery; I haven't weeded anything in several months. The lavender I planted is brittle and dead; the Mexican primrose is hanging on, but not blooming, since I haven't watered this side garden for a while either.

A small purple flower catches my eye, and when I see the leaves, my breath catches in my throat. Violets. No, can't be. But, upon closer inspection of the leaves, I note that they, indeed, are violets. The leaves are plump green hearts, and the flowers have the distinct five-petaled shape of the little flowers. I bend down to smell them, the fresh, old-fashioned scent I remembered so well, And I immediately think of my mother. Violets were her favorite flower.

I pick one and take it to my mother-in-law, a woman who was born and raised in Ohio and who moved to San Diego in the 1950s.

"It's a violet!" she exclaims when I show it to her. "Where did you get it?"

I tell her it's from my garden.

"No," she shakes her head. "They don't grow here. I've never seen one in San Diego."

After doing a bit of research later, I find that one type of violet, a carmine violet with an old-fashioned scent, is called "Noeli," which just happens to be my nickname for my young son. Once again, my mom has managed to find the perfect gift, to do the perfect thing, and to remind me that it's the small things, not the big ones, that stay with us . . . like the scent of a carmine violet on a California Christmas morning.

—*Laura Preble*

A Second Helping of
Funeral Sandwiches

M om and I watch from the living room window as a horse-drawn hayrack brings four,
five, and then six loads of men in from the cornfields
for the noon dinner.

"I wish the day were over," she says and moves
to Dad's recliner on the other side of the room. She
says it's too hard to face the neighbors, too painful to talk with friends who will celebrate forty
and fifty years of marriage—celebrations she won't
experience.

But we need to acknowledge the hundred or so
farmers who've spent the morning harvesting our
corn crop. So I zip my coat and find hats and mittens
for my three-year-old and sixteen-month-old sons.
The October sun is bright but deceiving, the wind
gentle but cool. The boys ask—for what seems like
the hundredth time—when they can have a tractor

ride, then race to the Morton building, sensing that something important is taking place.

Dad's tractors have been moved, his tools hung on pegs; the floor has been swept and washed. The new layout—eight-foot tables, each surrounded by ten folding chairs—is eerily reminiscent of our church fellowship hall, where funeral sandwiches were served only two months earlier.

But instead of petite triangles of egg and chicken salad, today's sandwiches are hearty—the kind needed to sustain farmers for the rest of the workday. BBQs. Sloppy joes. Taverns. Maid-Rites. Loose meat sandwiches. The names differ depending on the Midwestern community, but they're all served with slotted spoons from white ceramic roasters. It takes two, maybe three, roasters to feed the hundred farmers who have volunteered equipment and time to help their neighbor.

The line for food stretches past the roasters to more than twenty choices of salads and a dozen desserts that Mom's friends have prepared. Eight women stand guard, dishing up sandwiches, removing empty bowls, and serving coffee. Lots of coffee.

The place hums with laughter, good-to-see-you handshakes, and slaps to the back—the talk probably as much about corn prices, hail damage, and land values as about my dad. Even neighbors who have feuded over land and rights-of-way for two generations tip their hats to each other.

My brother is standing with our new tenant, arms crossed over his chest in typical farmer fashion, even though he isn't one. I'm sure they're discussing how much grain to haul to town and how much to store here at home. I hope he's about done. I've been gone for thirteen years and have forgotten many of our neighbors' names. This thank-you job would be easier if I could simply follow him from table to table.

Unfortunately, it doesn't appear he'll be done "farming" soon. So the boys and I move toward the men in plaid shirts, hooded sweatshirts, and seed-corn advertising caps. Many simply nod and raise their Styrofoam cup to me. They don't remember much about me, either.

But at one table, a farmer says, "We're glad to do it. Rex would've done the same for me."

"You know," another says, "I coffeed with your dad that morning. He looked so good. I still can't believe he's gone."

A woman I recognize but can't name appears at my side. "Come have something to eat," she says. "And how about the boys? I'll bet they're hungry. How old are they now? Keeping you plenty busy, I'm sure. Your mom says you're able to stay home with them now—how nice. And how nice for her that you're only five hours away."

I respond as graciously as I can to the neighbor with no name, asking only generic questions of her life and her family.

My sons have spied the chocolate cake, and for a few moments, the food table provides a refuge, sheltering me from a barrage of questions, protecting me from my memories.

"Do you want red Jell-O or orange Jell-O?" I ask my oldest.

LuAnne, a neighbor with a name I do remember, offers them brownies.

Silently congratulating myself, I greet her by name and whisper, "Who was that woman I was just talking to?"

Her warm smile tells me she understands my uneasiness.

LuAnne had seen this neighbor-helping-neighbor generosity all her life. But it is ten years later, when I sit down to watch the videotape, before I realize what the day was really about.

You see, October 18, 1995, was a good corn-pickin' day in central Nebraska. The ground was dry and the breeze pleasant. Farmers know how precious a good corn-pickin' day is. They know how Mother Nature affects their lives, that they have no control over the amount of rain, wind, and sunshine they receive or when it occurs. They know how every hour in the field translates into money in the bank.

That day, for nearly ten hours, thirteen combines worked their way through our fields, and forty trucks, trailers, and wagons hauled the grain to the elevator. At the end of the day, all six-hundred acres had been harvested.

The harvest bee was more than a group of farmers spending the day in our fields. Dad's friends unselfishly gave us a piece of their hearts. As they drove away at the end of that long day, the headlights of their combines, tractor-trailers, and semi-trucks were a silent tribute from their fields to ours—and more meaningful than the procession from the church to the cemetery.

—Karna Converse

This story aired on Iowa Public Radio in 2005.

Entwined Forever

We always slept in a tangle of arms and legs. One morning, I woke up and he didn't. It was that simple.

My husband John had fallen in our paved driveway and hit his forehead. Since he was on an anticoagulant, he developed a world-class black eye and assorted bruises. He said he felt a little strange, but a phone call to his doctor reassured me that this was to be expected. If John still had troublesome symptoms the next morning, the doctor advised, I should bring him to the clinic.

Morning came. John was unresponsive. I called an ambulance but knew that this was, in fact, a futile gesture. John was in a profound coma and died four hours later. I had become a member of a club I never wanted to join.

For weeks, I functioned pretty well, taking care of the legal duties that follow a death in the family.

To my friends' amazement and praise, I attended events and meetings. Doing concrete tasks kept me from digesting the unimaginable.

But John's boots were still on the doormat, his winter jacket on the bench in the entry. I couldn't watch *Jeopardy*. Couldn't sit at the kitchen table. I wore his watch along with mine; they'd been purchased together about twenty years earlier.

Then, a bit more than three months after his sudden death, I shattered. Grief enveloped me like a stifling cloud. Nightmares, daily anxiety attacks, and memory lapses frightened me. I had lived and slept and worked side by side with my husband for twenty-seven years. We were more than a couple. We were a unit.

Now, decisions that would have been made with a give and take of insights and opinions were mine alone.

Should the acres of timothy be put into conservation practice or trust that the old farmer who cut the hay would continue to do so in the future?

Which car should I keep? Which garden tractor? What about the commercial property in town—sell it or continue to lease it? If a tenant left, who would check the heat in the winter? Could I pay the taxes and insurance without income from rent?

Despite my education and business experience, I was overwhelmed.

I sought the comradeship of a grief-support group. It didn't help. As it happened, all the other members had experienced the loss of loved ones who had been ill for long periods of time, years, in some cases. And they had prepared themselves as much as they could for the inevitable day. "Pre-grieving," it was called. I was alone in the phenomenon of "here tonight, gone in the morning."

I did learn that the stages of grief, so often quoted in magazines and in the monthly newsletters mailed by the funeral home, don't always have the decency to appear in their proper sequence. I also learned that sometimes, when you think you're done with a particular stage, it comes back for an encore.

Friends who lent support and understanding in the early months after John's death had gone on with their own lives and concerns. I was loath to continue affecting them with my sorrow.

I wondered why we had let slip the custom of dressing the bereaved in black. It serves as a warning to those approaching: This person may be fragile. This person may be weepy or short-tempered or beset by any of a variety of moods.

Then I found a counselor. It took several tries to find the right fit for me. She affirmed that it was okay to wear John's flannel shirts, to leave his boots on the mat, to be undecided about the disposition of his ashes. She was patient, quiet, and unperturbed by my all-consuming grief. The minute I entered her office, I would break down sobbing. It was a safe place to unload deep feelings.

She also told me that grief often does not "go away." In her words, "It may never get any better, but you will get better at coping with it."

That, alone, took away my feeling of guilt. That, after a full year, after passing the first wedding anniversary, the first birthday, the first New Year's Day Rose Bowl Parade on television, it was just as normal to be deeply in grief as it was to be simultaneously climbing out of it. After a full year, people around you expect you to be getting past your mourning. You expect it, too. Often. It's too much to expect.

That second year even has a name: "the lonely year." Indeed, a deep aloneness crept in. There were still days that I referred to as "burka days," when I would have been relieved to be shrouded from head to toe while venturing out into the world, not wanting to pass the time of day in conversation at the grocery store or library.

In time, my counselor led me to see and to really believe that John was not absent from my life. I could sit with him when I needed to make a decision. I could settle my anxious mind and focus my thoughts on the problem at hand. This exercise made space for his wisdom, still present in me, to give silent voice to his ideas.

Together, John and I decided to let the farmer continue harvesting the hay. If he stopped in a few years, that was the time to take the next step.

Together, after debating the pros and cons of the commercial property, we leased it so the tenant was responsible for utilities and maintenance.

Together, we hired a man to mow the lawn with his own equipment. I could mow it if I wanted to, but the pressure of taking over chores that were John's was lessened.

Each decision, especially those involving other people, was based on what I had learned about reasoning from the years we had shared business responsibilities.

And, gradually, I let go of the guilt at not being all-competent.

What at first seemed to be a psychological band-aid applied by my counselor has now become a way of life. I miss my husband every day. The long body pillow does not take his place at night, but it fills up space and is something to hug.

So much of John is still here. His practical and laid-back approach to life is entangled in my harum-scarum personality. My opiate in time of grief or anxiety is a whiff from his bottle of Old Spice after-shave or Prell shampoo.

I still wear his watch and mine together. His keeps more accurate time.

I am a writer. My first publications occurred in the year prior to his unexpected death. He supported and cheered me on in my new endeavor. He has contributed immensely to the experiences and views expressed in both my fiction and nonfiction.

"Can you control it?" he would ask if I complained about a tax increase or a hailstorm that had damaged our vegetable garden. "If not, take two aspirin and go on to the next thing."

I couldn't control the events leading to my husband's death, but now his spirit gently pushes me to go on to the next thing.

—Ann Vitale

Making Peace

As I walked down the corridor of the nursing home, I thought about the last time I had visited my grandmother. She was still living alone in her one-room studio apartment then and had greeted me at the door with a mouthful of ice. After letting me in, Nammaw, with her stooped shoulders, pasty-white skin, and dark circles under her eyes, had walked over to the kitchen sink and spit out the ice. She explained that crunching on ice cubes was the only way she could keep herself from smoking. A dirty ashtray sat on the end table next to her recliner, and I wondered how well the ice-cube deterrent was working.

Now, a cup of water with a sponge-tipped swab stuck in it sat on the side table next to the metal hospital bed where Nammaw lay dying. And I wondered if she craved a cigarette.

The hospice nurses used the swab to give Nammaw cool water, because she could no longer swallow from a cup or sip from a straw. They would soak the pink sponge with water and rest it on her lips, moistening the chapped surface, over and over. If her lips were slightly parted, they would insert the swab into her mouth and swish the tip back and forth on her tongue. Sometimes, Nammaw would close her lips around the swab and suck out the moisture.

I sat on the edge of Nammaw's bed and reached for the water cup. Lifting the swab from the cup, I dabbed my grandmother's dry lips with the wet pink sponge. When her mouth opened slightly, I gently inserted the swab and rested it in on her tongue. Instinctually, Nammaw closed her lips around the stick and slid her tongue back and forth on the sponge for a couple of seconds, her eyes opening into slits.

"I'm here, Nammaw," I said, hoping she would recognize my voice.

After her tongue released its grip on the sponge, I gently pulled it out, placed the swab back in the cup, and set the cup back on the table.

When I turned back to my grandmother, her eyelids had already lowered into deep sleep again. My own eyelids felt heavy.

I had flown across two states at an early hour to be there, and my body was beginning to feel it. Before my mother had left the nursing home that night, she'd suggested that I lay next to Nammaw if I got tired.

I moved my left leg onto the firm mattress and eased part of my right leg on. There was enough room for both of us on the bed if I lay on my side. So I turned to face Nammaw, trying not to disturb the sheet or blanket. Her lips had formed the shape of an O, and I could hear weak breaths coming in and out of her mouth.

When I was a little girl, Nammaw would wrap her arms around me and try to plant a wet kiss on my lips. I let her do it a few times, but the smell of tobacco on her tongue made it difficult for me to breathe. Nammaw had stopped giving full-mouth kisses after I'd told her the smell made me sick to my stomach. She'd seemed disappointed when I'd turned my head and offered a cheek for her to kiss instead.

Now, as I lay next to Nammaw, I stroked her hair. It was smooth against my fingertips. The salt and pepper coloring reminded me of a puppy she had gone on and on about when I was young, the dog she had pulled out of a small box and given the name "Happy" because he made her feel good when she petted him. That puppy grew no bigger than

Nammaw's lap, but for some reason the dog always preferred my grandfather. When Nammaw and Papa divorced, Happy remained in the white mobile home with Papa. Nammaw saw less and less of the dog after she went away to live with her seventy-year-old mother. I don't think Happy ever warmed up to Nammaw. Perhaps the dog had his doubts about a woman who shoved him in a box with barely enough room to breathe.

Did Nammaw know that I was lying beside her? Could she feel my hand stroking her silky hair away from her remarkably smooth face? For a woman of seventy-two who had been through years of inner turmoil and had smoked for most of her adult life, her skin had few wrinkles.

I wondered if she were dreaming while she slept so deeply, perhaps about people she had lost or those of us who were still with her. I wondered if her body was still hanging onto life for a reason.

When I was growing up, Nammaw would regale our family with stories of how she'd climbed a water tower as a little girl. She described how tall the tower had been, how narrow its metal ladder had been. I suspected the story was a myth, not because of the implausibility of a young girl doing such a thing but because Nammaw recited the tale as if it were a prized Shakespearean play. Her flamboyant style and the fact that all the grownups in the room rolled their eyes as she spoke made me distrustful of her stories, yet sad that she felt compelled to keep telling them.

More than anything, I had wanted not to turn out like Nammaw. All my life, I wanted to disown her for the mental illness she carried that could be passed on for generations. One minute, she would be parading around town in satiny blouses and over-done makeup. The next, she would be isolating her-self at home in an unwashed robe with nothing on underneath. Whoever hadn't inherited her illness was haunted by those who had it.

Suddenly, my eyes began to glisten with tears. Not scant tears that were shed out of respectful sym-pathy for a dying loved one. These were thick, sor-rowful tears of regret. Regret at not having called Nammaw on her birthday last year. Regret at hav-ing laughed at her behind her back ever since I was ten years old. Regret at once having wished she wasn't my grandmother. Regret that I despised her for so long because of her manic depression. Remorse welled up from a pool deep inside me and gushed out in tears that streaked my face and ran down my neck. Then, the words that had squeezed my heart and wrenched my stomach for decades came rush-ing out too. Like my tears, I could not control them. They spilled out of my mouth and filled the quiet room with a message that seemed to have been dictated by God himself.

"Oh, Nammaw," I sobbed. "It wasn't your fault, I know that now. I was wrong. I do love you; I've always loved you. It really wasn't your fault."

Lying beside my dying grandmother, I finally understood and accepted that she hadn't chosen manic depression for herself or for her loved ones. That realization filled me with calm, and all the negative feelings that I'd harbored for so long were replaced with compassion and unconditional love for my grandmother. In that moment, a radiant warmth began to pulsate between our two bodies, as if creating a bridge between our two souls, as we lay side by side, breathing in and out.

With trembling lips, I leaned over and tenderly kissed Nammaw's open mouth, feeling and tasting her breath on mine, flowing softly in and out. Inhale, exhale. Inhale, exhale.

As I lifted my lips from hers, Nammaw raised her eyebrows into high arches above her closed eyes.

My grandmother had heard me . . . and accepted my peace offering.

—*Shanna Bartlett Groves*

Always There

My father died slowly, one stroke at a time, over a period of fourteen years.

First, we learned to live with a dad who couldn't talk or walk as fast as he used to.

Then, we adjusted to a father who refused to write because his handwriting was so shaky. He had learned the Palmer method in school and had been proud of his penmanship, especially his signature. When it became wobbly, he resolutely declined to pick up a pen unless he had to sign something.

Next, we realized he could no longer remember things. Grandchildren's names. Places we had been. How to play Lotto. How to tie a tie.

By the third or fourth stroke, he had days when he didn't know any of our names—his four children, his wife. He had moments when he couldn't connect names and faces, couldn't place who we were to him.

He would look at my mother and say, "What's your name?"

She would roll her eyes and say, "Rosemary."

"Oh," he would perk up. "My wife is named Rosemary. But I haven't seen her in a long time."

She had, of course, changed in the sixty years they'd been married, and sometimes he was back in some decade when she still had dark hair.

Still, he was Dad, as warm and humorous as ever. It was clear that he loved his family. He tried to slip each of us a little cash, and he was always glad to see the four of us and his five grandchildren, even when he was unsure of who we were, exactly. We got used to identifying ourselves when we came in. "Hey, Dad, it's Sheila."

The last years were tougher. Though Dad looked good, he didn't think or function well. He couldn't drive and didn't understand why. He would sit in the front seat and offer directions to the driver—"Slow down here," and "Get in that other lane." He would say things like, "Next summer, I'm going to get back out on the golf course," even when it took two people, one on each of his arms, to get him up a few steps.

While watching a football game on television, he would tell us, weekend after weekend, how he tried out for the high school team but was so small that other players could just pick him up and move him out of the way. We listened in sadness. We knew the story. In the last year, he would rely on one of us to fill in the details as they slipped away from him.

My father, who used to be funny, used to be able to tell a story, used to be able to sell anybody anything, who always knew what to say, would pause for ten or fifteen seconds between words. His mind just couldn't find the right one. A simple anecdote could take him fifteen minutes to tell. We'd smile and wait, offering words we thought might fit.

But the more time we spent with him, like on the weeklong cruise we all took together, the harder it was for everybody. We had to watch our quick-witted father morph into an elderly soul who needed constant supervision. My mother had to watch the same green eyes that used to understand every nuance now stare blankly at her when she mentioned a name or a place. And my father—well, knowing he couldn't always remember the punch line, he told fewer and fewer stories.

He did everything at a very slow pace. He walked and talked and ate slower than anyone I had ever seen. Someone had to have a hand on his elbow anytime we faced a curb or a step. He needed an escort to the men's room.

My father, who had always been an easy-going and level-headed person, developed a stubborn streak. He denied he had diabetes and tried to sneak hard candies whenever he could. Denying him ice cream was the worst. Ice cream was his favorite dessert. He ate any brand, any flavor, any day, and only complained that the portions were too small. We gave in on the cruise and allowed him to order ice cream. An obliging waiter brought huge portions, and we struggled with existential questions: Is prolonging life the goal even if it means giving up all the things that make life pleasurable? Or is it better to live a shorter life happily, enjoying its finer things? Do we have the right to make that choice for another person? In Dad's case, a steady diet of sugar had disastrous effects on his memory, his speech, and his bladder.

Then, he decided he didn't like pizza, previously one of his favorite foods. He used to love taking us all to one of Detroit's finest pizzerias and presiding over our table of twelve. Now, at that same restaurant he ordered anything but pizza.

In a family of excitable Irish men and women, my father's ability to calm and to nurture us all was sorely missed as he lost his gifts of insight and words. Ever the optimist, he had been the one to shore up my mother after she lost both breasts to breast cancer and to assure all of us that it was just another bump in the road we would all get over.

He could talk to anyone about anything. At every event, we would seat him next to people who were hard to get along with, knowing he'd engage them in conversation and keep things on an even keel. He had the gift of blarney in the old Irish sense of it.

So, when the fifth stroke robbed him of his speech, it seemed especially cruel. For seventeen days he laid in intensive care, unable to open his eyes, unable to talk, and then he died. He was eighty-nine.

One side of my brain said, *Dad wouldn't want to live any longer like this. He's been gone for a long time.*

But I bristled whenever anybody said, "It's a blessing he died." *No!* I wanted to scream. *How can it be a blessing that such a good and kind human being has left us? How can it be a blessing if we have such a gaping hole in our family?*

We had a big Irish funeral. A bagpiper piped. We sang, "When Irish Eyes Are Smiling." We all participated in some way—reading the scripture at Mass, being a pallbearer, writing a eulogy, finding and displaying hundreds of old photos of Dad before the first stroke and even some of the good times we'd had with him since. We exchanged amused glances when the military honor guard—earned by his World War

II Navy years—struggled with the flag-folding at the cemetery. We threw crimson roses on top of a shamrock-decorated vault after it was lowered into the ground.

Sixty of us—family and close friends—went to my dad's favorite little Greek place for the funeral luncheon. We passed around a sheet of his favorite sayings, and then laughed and sniffed a bit as we told our favorite Dad stories—of summer days at the cottage, fall days at football stadiums, and every Sunday at church.

Then we all went home.

Now what? I wondered.

In the days that followed, I began to entertain a thought I once would have dismissed: *Do people who have such a close connection to us come back after they have gone?* I'd never believed that before. Now, my imagination refused to discount anything. *What if Dad came back? How would we know?*

Seven weeks after the funeral, all three of my children came home for Thanksgiving. They don't look anything like my father. Our two sons are at least four inches taller and neither is barrel-chested. None of my kids has my father's red hair or intense green eyes. But they are old enough to remember their grandfather before his first stroke. My father spent hours with each one, telling them stories about his parents, teaching them to skip rocks in Lake Huron, taking them out to eat or to church, cooking breakfast for them, taking them to the cemetery where his grandparents are buried. He was always there, a part of the fabric of their lives.

I began to see bits of him in the ways my children analyzed a problem or reacted to a crisis or told a story. His sense of humor was still alive, I could see, in them. His expressions popped out of their mouths and on their faces. His thrifty shopping skills and his love of newspapers had been passed down to my kids as well. *Is this the way people come back,* I wondered. *In their grandchildren?*

When the three kids came home for Christmas, it was our daughter who bought us tickets to a basketball game at his favorite college—something he would have relished. He'd taken me to games on campus long before she was born or enrolled there. He'd taught me how to sell extra tickets—always keep a tight grip on one end when you show the seat row and number to the prospective buyer.

My job was to park the car while the others went in, a tough task in Ann Arbor. We were late, and all the nearby streets and paid lots were full. Maybe, I thought, I could park in a lot I knew from football Saturdays when our kids were in the marching band. I whipped around the now deserted streets and found the lot, only half full because most of the students were gone for winter vacation. Still, I didn't have a permit, so I drove out of the lot through the back exit and found an alley I had never been down.

An unfamiliar sense of excitement and daring filled me. I was soon on a two-lane rut behind the softball fields, wondering if this path was meant for cars. But it was too narrow to turn around and I didn't want to anyway. Something else was driving me. I wanted to see where the dirt path went and I wanted to find a space to park the car. Suddenly, I saw the basketball arena across a tiny bridge from a parking lot with empty spaces. I pulled in. A free parking space. Heh heh heh.

As I walked toward the arena, I passed signs stating that this, too, was a permit-only lot. I analyzed the situation: The game was half over. It was winter vacation. I was parked at the extreme end of the lot, surrounded by maintenance trucks. I decided to risk it.

"Where are you parked?" my husband asked when I found the seats.

"Illegally," I said, watching his eyes widen at something so unusual.

Suddenly, I knew it was the same thing Dad would have done. He'd been a master at finding back alleys and less-than-legal parking places that somehow worked for him. I was not. I am as square as they come. I plug meters with extra coins. I pay for parking garages, winding up and up ramps until I find an open space. I drive around city blocks looking for the right parking spot and then walk miles back to my destination. I always park legally. But not this time. This time I pulled it off, and I didn't get a ticket. It was as if something else in me, something that had been in me all along, took over.

The months of grieving took their toll; I was emotionally and physically exhausted. So my husband booked the two of us on a five-day cruise for the first week in January.

On the ship, we chuckled at how Dad loved to play Bingo on the cruises he had taken and how he had won the big jackpot once. Characteristically, he'd given each of us $100 from the pot.

My husband bought Bingo cards for four games one rainy afternoon. They came with a free card for the fifth game, the hardest to win because it required covering every square on the card, but it had the biggest pot of the afternoon—$124. We sat side by side, each with our own card for that last game, remembering Dad, following the caller, watching the spaces on our cards fill up as we got closer to the big pot. Then I was only one number away from Bingo. By the ship's rules, I had to stand up.

"Okay, Dad, here we go," I muttered, standing alone in the room, feeling not so alone.

The steward called the next number. Someone else stood up; now two of us were only one number away from Bingo. *It figures*, I thought. *I never win anything.*

The steward called two or three more numbers. None mine. Still more people stood up.

Another number rang out. Bingo! I won!

Some people would say their father had a hand in that. Some would make a big deal out of how they'd come full circle, how the memories of the dad who stumbled on curbs and searched for words and conversed less and less with the family he loved had been replaced with memories of the Dad who walked every night for exercise, swinging a thick stick to strengthen his arms, who deftly handled difficult people, and who taught us everything we needed to survive in the world. Parking a car. Winning at Bingo.

That would be me.

—Sheila O'Brien Schimpf

Through Loss Comes
the Greatest Gift

It's been twenty-three years since my mother surrendered to metastatic breast cancer at the age of forty-seven. I was seventeen when she died, and it seems impossible to consider that I've been remembering her—conjuring her sweet smile and big green eyes in my mind, telling the taller-by-the-year tales of her Italian temper, praying for her guidance—longer than I actually knew her.

I loved her terribly, but I'd forgotten how to tell her so. During the five years after her diagnosis, I had made a science of coolly detaching myself from the ugly mess that was my life. I was young and stupid and angry.

In the spring of 1986, my father moved us from our home in Florida to that of his younger sister, Jeanette, in Connecticut. We stowed our possessions in a rented storage shed and settled as best as we could into Jeanette's dark paneled basement, which had variegated-brown shag carpeting that made it look like it was built on the back of a big dog. Between the paisley velour sectional and the console television we wedged the bed in which my mother would pass every single day of the rest of her life—minus time spent hunched before the toilet in the bathroom down the hall, vomiting from the chemotherapy that was supposed to save her.

Our dog, a smart, formerly spoiled shepherd mix named Samantha, now spent her days on the wrong side of the back door, carving a half-circle in the grass at the end of a chain. In separating Samantha and my mother, Jeanette had relieved each of one of her few remaining pleasures—the other's company. I despised her for it.

The day my mother slipped into a seizure before my eyes, weeks before her death, we were chatting aimlessly—about the school play I was doing and the cadre of misfits I was doing it with, about my part-time job lugging flats of flowers and bales of peat moss at a nearby garden center, about the car I hoped to buy. We never spoke of her health or of our living conditions or of the future. I sat in my familiar spot on her bed, and she was where she always was, propped up by a mountain of pillows and tethered to an oxygen tank by a clear tube looped over her ears and under her nose, her small legs stretched out beneath the covers and hands by her sides. Her voice was light as a feather by then, nearly gone; she spoke in a fluttery, gurgly soprano that belied the roaring mouth I remembered so clearly from a hundred years before, when life was normal. My father was nearby, unshaven and rumpled as he always seemed to be during that time, and Jeanette was there, too, doing whatever it was she did—hovering, loitering, perching like an owl on a dying person's rooftop. Before the event began, with the harmless and puzzling stir of a finger, the afternoon was no different from dozens that had come before it—bleak and, with any luck, forgettable.

The index finger of my mother's right hand began to move, soft and steady, as if tapping along to one of those terrible Pointer Sisters songs to which she used to pace her fitness walks way back when. She was amused at first, and I think I was, too, to watch the strumming contractions of her finger. She shook her head at this latest bodily malfunction, reminded yet again of what a high-mileage misfit she'd become. But the twitching gathered intensity, and as it did, her expression stiffened from soft amusement to alarm. The thrumming in her knobbly index finger had now commandeered her whole hand and was fast moving up her arm before it caught the attention of my father from across the room. In the eternal seconds it took for him to arrive at her side, the beating contractions of the seizure had swallowed her to the shoulder.

"Oh, Paul!" she cried out, eyes wild with fear, as the seizure that was engulfing her body swept into her neck and across her face.

My father instructed me to call 911 and get an ambulance.

"I think my mother's having a seizure," I said into the phone.

Over my shoulder, the woman who'd given me life had been pinned to the bed in an effort to save her from her thrashing, a leather belt slotted between her teeth to spare her lips and tongue. I replaced the phone handset and bolted up the short flight of stairs and out the front door.

I sat on the stoop, useless but at least out of the way. And I waited. Life in the neighborhood carried on as if nothing was happening. A lawnmower rattling here, a basketball bouncing there. *How dare they? Didn't they know that through these dingy basement windows, a good woman—my beloved mother—was dying? Was it too much to ask for a little respect?*

And then it came. Far off in the distance, the howl of a siren arrived on the breeze, singing of running red lights and weaving through afternoon traffic. But the neighborhood remained unmoved. The wail grew louder, closer, rounding the far corner now, ringing in my ears and filling my chest. Louder. Louder still. Now here. Right here in front of me, garish lights flashing away. I stood. The siren stopped mid-whoop; the sudden silence created a vacuum that pulled my eardrums outward.

I stepped aside for the two paramedics as they strode through the front door and down into the basement. I said nothing to them and I didn't follow. I looked out over the lawns and driveways and discovered a neighborhood newly unified in the task of gawking. Catching a glimpse of somebody else's bad day. From inside open garages and behind hedges and through picture windows, neighbors I'd never met watched as this great and lurid melodrama unfolded across the street.

When it was over and the ambulance was gone and the neighbors had gone back to whatever it was they'd been doing before the excitement, I sat again with my mother, who was sedated now or perhaps simply exhausted. Sweaty and sunken into her pillows, she held my hand in hers—the same hand that had started this nightmare an hour before.

And with tears heavy in her gigantic eyes, she drew a breath and, to my complete befuddlement, apologized for doing this to me. "I'm so sorry, Matthew," she whispered. "I'm so sorry."

I shared this story not long ago with my wife of three years, who wears my mother's wedding band and with whom I recently embarked on the terrifying, magnificent journey of parenthood. She wept when she heard it.

"That's a mother's love," she said through her tears. "To go through such pain, to suffer that way, and still care only for your child. To want him to be okay. That's the pure love of a mother."

It was at that moment that these two women who'd never met—one lost to cancer in 1986 and one who now holds her granddaughter—became linked forever. The pain and selflessness of the first and the insight and heart of the second had merged and revealed to me a higher truth. The highest truth, in fact. They have given me new ways to love them both and taught me the only way to love my children—completely.

—*Matthew Phenix*

Contributors

Nancy Antonietti ("The Dark Green") is a retired engineer from New Hampshire who has been expressing herself through writing since she can remember. Her writing has been published in *Strut Magazine, Americal Journal, The New Hampshire Mirror,* and in *The Fray.* She is currently working on a novel while caring for an adorable husband, three precious sons, and two geriatric Labrador retrievers.

Louise Beech ("The Strongest Link") writes for love. She wrote a newspaper column for seven years, has published short fiction in numerous magazines, and is currently studying playwriting. Her stories are inspired by her two children, one husband, five pets, travel, the ocean, and her voluntary work with children in care.

Marcia E. Brown ("Gifts of Grace") is an Austin, Texas, freelance writer who began writing family stories fifteen years ago to preserve them for her family. She has been widely published in magazines, newspapers, and anthologies, including several *Cup of Comfort®* anthologies. She is a member of the National League of American Pen Women and Writers' League of Texas.

Priscilla Carr ("My Ever Muse") is a memoirist and poet from Nottingham, New Hampshire, and founder of the New Hampshire Poets Studio. Her essays appear in *A Cup of Comfort® for Dog Lovers, My Dog*

Is My Hero, and *My Teacher Is My Hero;* her poetry appears in various literary journals and in *It Has Come to This: The Poets of the Great Mother Conference.*

Loy Michael Cerf ("Gone Fishing"), an animal-loving, Chicago-area freelance writer, enjoys making blankets for Project Linus and dreaming up creative ways to coerce her grown children into pet-sitting so that she might travel the world with her husband of thirty-something years.

SuzAnne C. Cole ("Bending, Not Breaking), a mother, grandmother, traveler, retired college English instructor, and award-winning writer, has published more than 350 poems, essays, short stories, and articles in commercial and literary magazines, anthologies, and newspapers. She's pleased to have been included in two other *Cup of Comfort*® anthologies.

Karna Converse ("A Second Helping of Funeral Sandwiches") is a freelance writer whose essays have appeared in the *Christian Science Monitor, Notre Dame Magazine,* the *Cup of Comfort*® as well as other anthologies, *Our Iowa,* and on Iowa Public Radio. She lives in Storm Lake, Iowa, with her husband and their three children.

Myrna Courtney ("Some Small Joy") lives in Grass Valley, California. For about twenty-five years of their marriage, she and her husband Gerry traveled and published articles in various magazines, with Myrna writing and Gerry contributing the photography. "Joy" has become part of their family motto, keeping Gerry in their hearts and in their daily lives.

Amy Crofford ("Don't Be Brave") is a freelance writer and missionary. She has authored missionary books for children and adults. Her family has lived in France, the Côte d'Ivoire, Benin, Haiti, and numerous places in the United States. Currently, Amy and her husband live in Kenya.

Paula v.Wende Dáil ("The Ring") is a visiting research scholar at the University of Wisconsin, Milwaukee, where she is writing a monograph on women in poverty. Widely published in the social sciences, she has also received awards for both her academic and more creative writing endeavors. She divides her time between Menomonee Falls and Mineral Point, Wisconsin.

Karen Ferrick-Roman ("To Infinity and Beyond") is an award-winning writer living in Beaver Falls, Pennsylvania. She enjoys the quiet of a campfire, the calmness of kayaking, and the conversation of a good party. Though she takes special pleasure in beating her husband at cribbage, her passions revolve around travel and family.

Amber Frangos ("Hospice for the Holidays") is a freelance writer residing in Kentucky. Her publishing credits include fiction, nonfiction, and poetry. When she is not writing, she keeps busy helping her husband renovate their farmhouse while trying to dodge the eggs laid by her free-range chickens.

Sally Friedman ("Her House Was in Order"), a graduate of the University of Pennsylvania, contributes personal essays to the *New York Times,* the *Philadelphia Inquirer,* and anthologies. A New Jersey resident, she is the mother of three, grandmother of seven, and wife of a New Jersey Superior Court Judge.

Pat Gallant ("So Soft Her Goodbye") is a fourth-generation New Yorker, wife, mother of one son, daughter of two professional writers, and award-winning writer. Her work has appeared in the *Saturday Evening Post* and *Writer's Digest* as well as in *A Cup of Comfort® for Christmas, A Cup of Comfort® for Writers, Family Gatherings, Letters to My Mother, Things That Go Bump in the Night,* and other anthologies.

Esther Griffin ("Just One") is a retired special education teacher, school library media specialist, and coordinator of Educational Central Services. She has had a few magazine articles published in the past, and as a zoo docent for twenty-four years, she has written three animal books, as yet unpublished. Esther was widowed in 1996.

Ona Gritz ("The Part That Stays") is a prize-winning poet and the author of two children's books. Her essays have been published widely, including in other *Cup of Comfort®* anthologies. In 2007, she received two Pushcart nominations, and in 2008, she placed second for the

Bellingham Reviews' Annie Dillard Award for Creative Nonfiction. She writes a monthly column for the online journal, *Literary Mama.*

Rebecca Groff ("Believe, Persevere, Continue") lives in Cedar Rapids, Iowa. A freelance writer, she has published in national and regional magazines, anthologies, and online literary journals and recently completed a novel, *Iron Angel.* She gets her best writing done while communing with nature.

Shanna Bartlett Groves ("Making Peace") has contributed stories to several *Cup of Comfort®* books and is the author of the novel *Lip Reader.* Based in Kansas, Shanna frequently writes about being a hard-of-hearing mother to three young children as well as hearing loss issues.

Nancee Harrison ("Aunt Nancee Danced") lives in Greenwood, Indiana, but keeps close ties with family and friends in Dugger. She and her husband, Steven Jackson, both enjoy traveling. A freelance writer and past columnist for several different newspapers in Indiana, she has published fiction and nonfiction articles in numerous national magazines. She no longer "Shuffles Off to Buffalo."

Jan Henrikson ("A Wink and a Moo") writes, edits, and hikes in Tucson, Arizona. She and her boyfriend ride through the mountains on his Harley, sending love to her mom, who always dreamed of riding a motorcycle. She is editor of Sylvia Haskvitz's book, *Eat by Choice, Not by Habit.*

Amy Hudock, PhD, ("Carolina Blue") the founding co-editor of LiteraryMama.com, teaches English at an independent college prep school in South Carolina, where she lives with her daughter. She is the co-editor of *Literary Mama: Reading for the Maternally Inclined* and *American Women Prose Writers, 1820–1870.* Her work—which includes scholarly articles, essays, and fiction—has been published in numerous publications, including *Cup of Comfort®, Skirt!,* and *Pregnancy and Baby.*

Christine Jelley ("The Way We Were") is a freelance writer who resides on Long Island, New York, where she owns a surge protection manufacturing company. When she's not fighting transient over-voltages, she is enjoying time with her two sons, Ed and Chris, and their dog, Dave.

Kimila Kay ("Burying Bea") balances her love of writing with meeting the needs of her investment-company clients. She lives with her husband Randy, and Boston terrier, Maggie, in Portland, Oregon. Her first published essay appears in A *Cup of Comfort® for Single Mothers*. Kimila is a member of Willamette Writer's and Rose City Romance Writer's.

Candy Killion ("Winks from Heaven") is a freelance writer who has contributed to several anthologies, including *Cup of Comfort®*. She is the 2005 recipient of the Chistell Poetry Prize. She and her husband John live in Hollywood, Florida, with their spoiled Belgian Malinois dog, Hannah.

Jean Kinsey ("A Fitting Farewell"), a retired realtor, mother of three, and grandmother of seven, lives in Brooks, Kentucky. She is active in her church, where she teaches Sunday school. Her short stories have been published in anthologies and periodicals. She is currently writing a historical inspirational novel.

Marybeth Lambe ("Hope") is a family physician, author, and mother of eight children. She lives with her family on a small farm outside Seattle, in Washington State.

Andrea Langworthy ("Paying Homage") is a columnist for the *Rosemount Town Pages* and *Minnesota Good Age* newspapers and an instructor at the Loft Literary Center in Minneapolis. Her work has appeared in anthologies, including *The Ultimate Christmas*, as well as in numerous regional magazines.

Rachel McClain ("Alone in a Crowd") lives in Los Angeles but loves everywhere the Air Force sends her family. She has been published as a prize-winning author in *Women on Writing*. She has also been published in *Tuesday Shorts, Everyday Fiction, Fuselit, One Page Stories, Mom Writer's Literary Magazine*, and three other *Cup of Comfort®* anthologies.

Laurie McConnachie ("In My Own Time") lives in Seattle with her husband and son. She holds B.A. and M.A. degrees from Stanford University. Her writing has been published locally and nationally, including in *A Cup of Comfort® for Families Touched by Alzheimer's* and *Voices of Caregiving*. Her essay in this book is dedicated to her beautiful mother.

Carolyn McGovern ("So Far and Yet So Near") is a retired probation officer who lives in Manalapan, New Jersey, with her husband. Her work has been published in the *Shine Journal, Storyglossia, Chick Lit Review, Fly in Amber, Clever,* and others. She is currently at work on her memoir.

Lindsay Nielsen ("Gifts"), a writer and psychotherapist, lives with her husband and youngest son in Minneapolis, Minnesota. Her son Miles is now grown, with a son of his own. Fourteen luminaries are still put out every New Year's Eve in memory of her son Josh. She is writing a memoir and published an essay in *Good Housekeeping* magazine.

Janet Oakley ("Putting Things Away") has been published in several *Cup of Comfort®* anthologies and online at HistoryLink.org. Her essay "Drywall in the Time of Grief" (in *A Cup of Comfort® Classic Edition*) was the top winner in nonfiction at the Surrey International Writers Conference, 2006. Currently, she is writing an historical novel about the nineteenth-century Pacific Northwest. Her brown dog, Mocha, keeps her on track.

Matthew Phenix ("Through Loss Comes the Greatest Gift") is the deputy editor for *Caribbean Travel + Life* magazine. He started his writing career at the *New York Times* and has since contributed to a host of magazines, including *Wired, Popular Science, The Robb Report,* and *Automobile*. He now lives in Florida with The Girls: wife Jerri Anna, daughter Audrey, and dog Maggie.

Annelies Pool ("Family Spilling Over") is a freelance writer, columnist, and editor of the Northern Canadian inflight magazine *above&beyond, Canada's Arctic Journal*. She works out of her home in a cabin in the boreal forest, about twenty miles outside Yellowknife, Northwest Territories, Canada.

Laura Preble ("Violets Aren't Blue"), a writer and a teacher, is the author of a young adult novel series, *Queen Greek Social Club* (Penguin) and the winner of the 2005 Kurt Vonnegut Fiction Prize. A native of Lima, Ohio, she lives with her husband, jazz musician Chris Klich, and sons Austin and Noel, in San Diego, California.

Rosemary Rawlins ("My Father Heard Music") is a freelance writer for local nonprofit organizations. She lives in Glen Allen, Virginia, with her husband Hugh, twin daughters Mary and Anna, and her beloved mother Jule. Rosemary has been a caregiver for both of her parents, but knows she has received far more from them than she could ever give.

Mary Lou Reed ("Heading Home") is a writer/editor living in Torrance, California. She has been editor of *California Diving News*, a scuba diving publication, for the past twenty-five years and is a regular contributor to *Guideposts* magazine. Surrounded by her loving family, including eight grandchildren, she keeps busy writing and painting.

Mary Rudy ("More Than a Dream") lives outside San Francisco with her husband, two children, and two dogs. Her fiction has appeared in *Writer's Digest, Pisgah Review,* and *Coe Review,* and she has an essay in *A Cup of Comfort® for Dog Lovers II.*

Sheila O'Brien Schimpf ("Always There") is a freelance writer and former newspaper reporter. For twelve years she wrote a weekly column about family life, including raising her three children. She lives in East Lansing, Michigan, with her husband and four golden retrievers.

Christina Smith ("See What You Need") resides in Dunedin, Florida, with her husband Cameron and two-year-old twin boys Grayson and Hayden. In between chasing after toddlers and writing, she's a marketing specialist for YourMembership.com. A contributor to *A Cup of Comfort® for Women in Love,* she is currently working on a novel. She continues to see her father whenever she needs.

Kate Tapper ("Hit") lives in South Bend, Indiana, with her two children. She teaches at her sons' school and also freelances. She hopes to get an MFA in creative writing and either write the great American novel or teach what she loves most: reading and writing. Either scenario would make her mom very proud.

Susan B. Townsend ("Not Good at Goodbyes") is a stay-at-home mother and writer who lives on a farm in southeastern Virginia with her husband and five children. She is the author of *A Bouquet for Mom* and *A Bouquet for Grandmothers*, the editor or co-editor of several Christian volumes of the *Cup of Comfort*® book series, and a contributing author to numerous *Cup of Comfort*® anthologies.

Ann Vitale ("Entwined Forever") lives in Montrose, Pennsylvania. A former microbiologist, dog trainer, 4-H leader, and Ford dealer, she shares her rural home with her Newfoundland. She has been published in both short fiction and nonfiction anthologies and currently teaches and coaches writing at adult schools and cultural centers in several counties.

Davi Walders ("Calling Out for Angels") developed and directs the Vital Signs Writing Project at the National Institute of Health in Bethesda, Maryland. A recipient of numerous writing fellowships, this award-winning writer and poet's work has appeared in more than 200 anthologies and journals, read by Garrison Keillor on *Writer's Almanac*, and performed in New York City and elsewhere.

Kelly Wilson ("Floating Questions, Holding Life"), a busy mother and writer, has been creating characters and stories since she was in elementary school. She currently lives with her husband and two small children in Portland, Oregon.

About the Editor

Colleen Sell has compiled and edited more than thirty volumes of the *Cup of Comfort*® book series. A veteran writer and editor, she has authored, ghost-written, or edited more than 100 books and served as editor-in-chief of two award-winning magazines. She and her husband, T.N. Trudeau, live in a turn-of-the-century farmhouse on a forty-acre pioneer homestead in the Pacific Northwest.